Ruts, Guts, & a Model T Truck

Ruts, Guts, & a Model T Truck

Cruising the West at 15 Miles per Hour

R. KENT CRAWFORD

Some photos included here appeared in *A Year in the West: A Kansas Family's Expedition,* 2000. Used by permission.

Cover Design by BespokeBookCovers.com

ISBN: 978-0-578-79746-5

Library of Congress Control Number: 2020923653

POST
ROCK
PRESS
KNOXVILLE, TN

Post Rock Press
Knoxville, Tennessee

The most important reason for going from one place to another is to see what's in between.
　　—Norton Juster

Stop worrying about the potholes in the road and enjoy the trip.
　　—Babs Hoffman

Contents

Route of Crawford Trip

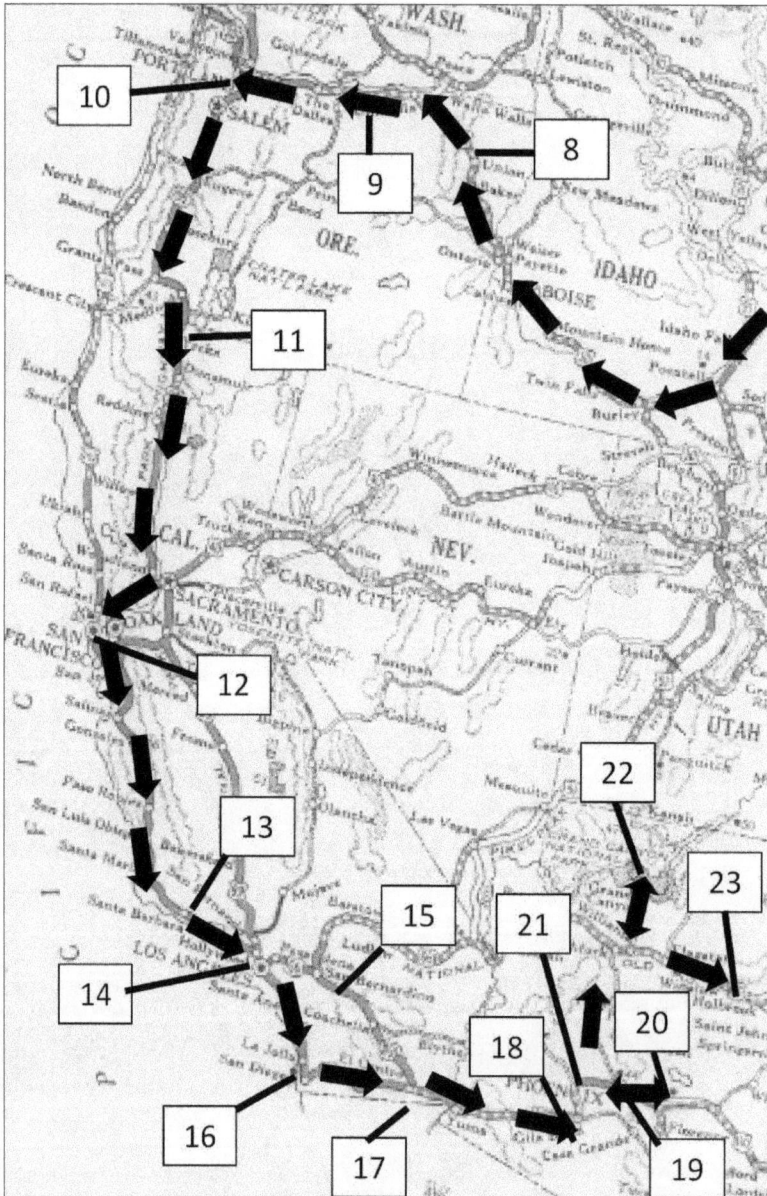

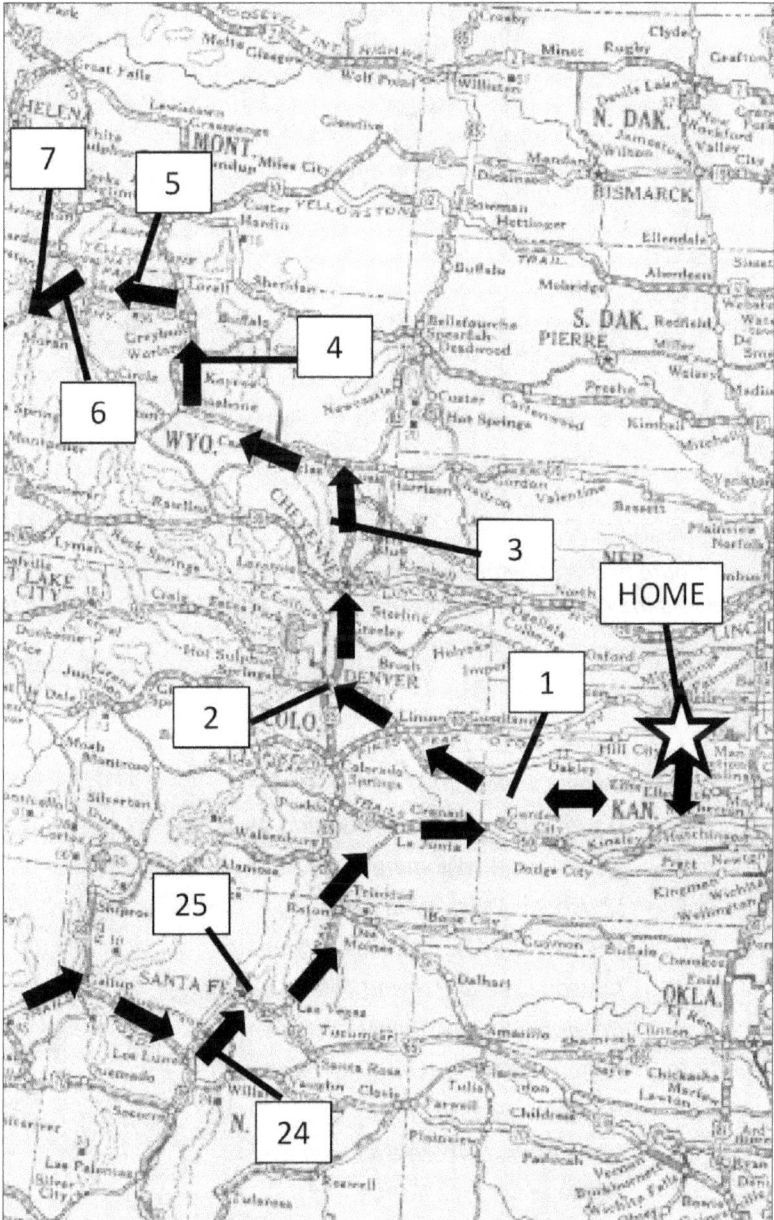

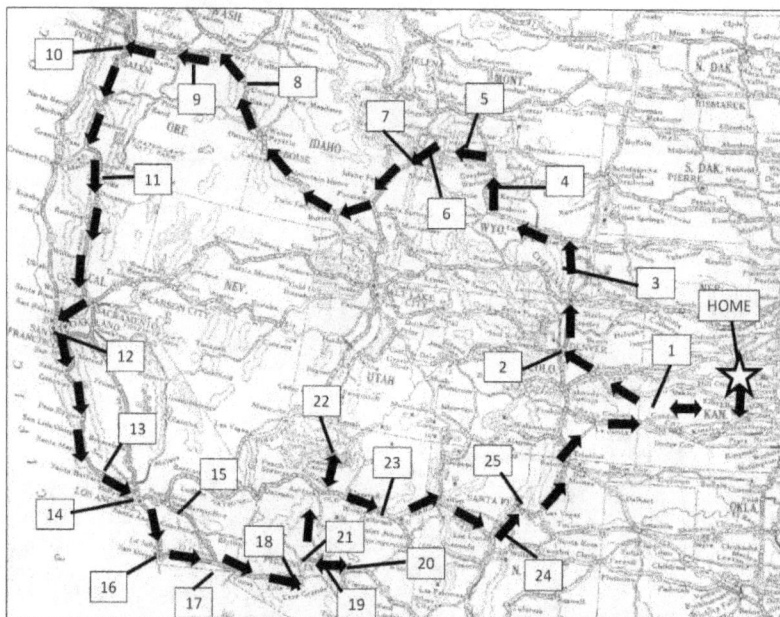

1. Route of the Crawford trip, indicating the locations of some of the places they visited. (Map courtesy of 1927 Rand McNally Road Atlas)

⭐ Home

1. Robert Beach Family
2. Denver, Colorado
3. Bradley Johnson Family, Glendo, Wyoming
4. Thermopolis, Wyoming
5. Shoshone Dam, Wyoming
6. Yellowstone National Park, Wyoming
7. Jackson Lake and Grand Tetons, Wyoming
8. Columbia Plateau wheat farm, Oregon
9. Columbia River Highway, Oregon
10. Portland, Oregon
11. Hornbrook, California salmon weir
12. San Francisco, California

A Journey

into History

A Mysterious Album about a Remarkable Trip

A trip to the attic is always a journey into history—sometimes dull and boring history, but occasionally something extraordinary. One can never tell where such a journey might lead. This book is the result of one such journey.

My father, Clarence Crawford, had a noteworthy attic filled with a lifetime of accumulations, ranging from items that passed down from his parents and grandparents to childhood mementos of my sister and me, including a multitude of items spanning the intervening years. Access to his attic was challenging, to say the least, requiring the use of a ladder to climb up through a small hatchway in the ceiling of a closet while dodging a protruding lightbulb along the way. I think Dad preferred it this way, since the difficulty of access kept my mother away from the attic, protecting Dad's accumulated artifacts from her periodic bouts of contributions to garage sales. The tortuous access helped create an aura about that attic, like entering a special new world, and a trip there was always enlightening and well worth the effort.

This time, while looking for something else, I came across an old photo album. My previous experiences with old family albums suggested that this album would also be filled with unlabeled pictures of long-deceased family members totally unknown to me, and hence of little interest. Imagine my surprise upon opening the album, and instead, finding pictures of hydroelectric dams, seashore beaches, battleships, an ocean liner, and other scenes remote from anything to be found in, or even near, where my parents lived in Kansas. The mystery of this album had me hooked.

2. Typical page from the Crawford album. Individual photos, most with no captions, were glued in spaces wherever they fit, with each album page usually including photos from several unrelated places.

Fortunately, my father, then in his 80s, knew the source of this album. It turns out that in 1922, his parents Roy and Albina Crawford took their two children, Clarence and Pauline, and left their farm in Kansas to go on a nearly-year-long camping trip through the West. This album contained the photographs taken on that trip. Shortly after learning this, my wife, Charlotte, and I interviewed Clarence and Pauline, recorded their remembrances of the trip, collected comments from my sister Candace Crawford, and published these remembrances and comments for family members along with a few of the identifiable pictures as *A Year in the West: A Kansas Family's Expedition.* Clarence and Pauline were respectively seven and nine years old at the time of that trip, and their memories of that time were limited. Furthermore, only a few of the photos in the album were readily identifiable, leaving the subjects and locations for most of the photos and hence the knowledge of most of the details of that trip still a mystery.

This mystery kept nagging, finally culminating in a dedicated effort to decipher the photos, an effort not completed until nearly two decades after the initial retrieval of the album from Dad's attic. Finally, I was able to finish my own journey into this history and remove much of the remaining mystery, bringing more of this remarkable trip to light.

The album from Dad's attic contained 270 photographs taken on this trip, and Pauline had saved numerous post cards they had collected from some of the places they had been. The Crawfords had written captions on some of the pictures in the album, but the majority of the pictures they took were never labeled.

Now, nearly 100 years after that trip, I have carried out my own detective work on these pictures and post cards along with Dad and Aunt Pauline's remembrances, and have determined most of the path followed and the places visited by the Crawfords. Mapping out the trip itinerary often required considerable internet research to determine just what the subjects were and where each picture was taken. I then used my best judgement to fill in a few gaps and to piece together a more nearly complete description of the route they took, the many places they visited, and some of what they did. This book, which includes many of the trip pictures or edited portions of them, along with a narrative describing the trip, is the result.

According to Pauline and Clarence, Albina had been suffering from serious respiratory problems in the early 1920s. During the winter of 1921-22, the doctor told her that she needed to spend some time in a warm dry climate (a common belief at that time[1]) away from the harsh Kansas winters. Upon hearing this, Roy began planning a trip for the Crawfords to spend the next winter in Southern California.

---

[1] Since that time, medical research has shown that cold dry winter air stresses respiratory systems, and that warm sunny climates can be beneficial provided they are relatively clear of allergens and air pollution.

I know that Roy loved farming, so the decision to leave their farm behind for nearly a year must have been a difficult one. However, he always liked to visit new places and to see how other people lived and he decided that although the trip was primarily for Albina's health, he and the family would make the most of it. The route they planned and then travelled certainly did this, turning into a 10+ month, 5,300-mile (not counting side trips) camping trip through the West.

Their route passed through eight different states and they stopped for stays of various lengths in most of them. This trip spanned elevations ranging from over 8,000 feet above sea level to nearly 200 feet below sea level and took the family through mountainous, heavily forested, and desert landscapes to the shores of the Pacific Ocean; all distinct from the nearly treeless, gently rolling prairie of central Kansas.

A trip of this magnitude, visiting all of these places, would be challenging even today. One can only imagine what guts it must have taken for the Crawfords to embark on such a trip in 1922, leaving their home to travel and live for most of a year in a vehicle that could average no more than about fifteen miles per hour. They must have known that they would have to improvise frequently, given the uncertain reliability of the vehicle, the roads, and the support facilities along the way. However, such a trip may not have seemed so daunting to Roy and Albina, whose parents had had the optimism, self-confidence, and fortitude to uproot their families and travel significant distances to uncertain futures carving out farms on the harsh Kansas plains only a few decades earlier. The idea of spending a year living with few amenities, camping and maintaining their vehicle during their travels, may not have seemed to Roy and Albina to be such a hardship, but more of an educational adventure.

The pictures from their trip, nearly one hundred years old by the time of this writing, tell most of the story of this trip; what they saw and experienced, what the travel was like, what the people wore and how they lived on the trip, and what activities were of interest in those locales at that time. Most places they experienced and things they saw have undergone enormous changes since 1922, and notes about some of these changes appear throughout this book. Improved highways and higher-speed vehicles make travel far different now from the low-speed experience it was then. Perhaps even more striking is how much more crowded many of the places are now than they were in 1922, especially the National Parks, other tourist spots, and urban areas throughout Southern California, Arizona, and New Mexico. Many of the sights the Crawfords saw have changed significantly with time, and in a number of cases, those sights no longer exist. For all these reasons, it would be impossible for a modern traveler to have the kinds of experiences evident in the pictures from the Crawfords' trip, even if they were to try to retrace the route taken by the Crawfords in 1922-23.

Preparations for the Trip

Background information about the Crawford family and their Kansas farm in the 1920s suggests that the idea of making such a trip might not be as outlandish as it first seemed. The Crawfords, Roy, Albina, Pauline, and Clarence, lived on a wheat farm in a community of farms in the vicinity of the Amherst Church and country school. This Amherst community is near the small town of Luray in central Kansas in the middle of the Great Plains.

Roy Crawford's parents had come from Pennsylvania and homesteaded on this land in 1879, and Roy was born there in 1882. In 1904, Roy purchased land of his own, adjacent to his parents' homestead. Roy married Albina Hampl in 1908. She was born in Nebraska in 1887, and in 1897, she traveled with her parents and siblings in a covered wagon to a farm about three miles from the Crawford farm in central Kansas. After they were married, Roy and Albina first lived in a small house next to Roy's parents, but Roy began to build a new house and outbuildings on the land he had purchased earlier. Their first child, Pauline, was born in the small house in 1913, but later that year Roy, Albina, and Pauline moved into the new house that would be their residence for the remainder of their lives. Their second child, Clarence, was born in that new house in 1915.

Roy was an excellent farmer and an astute businessman. He was also a first-rate mechanic, repairing his machinery as needed and using his machining and blacksmithing skills to build replacement components when necessary. Born the third of six surviving children in his family, Roy was the oldest boy and assumed many responsibilities at an early age. When he was seven years old, his family, faced with drought on the farm, retreated from their homestead in central Kansas to the Kansas City area in eastern Kansas to earn some money and to allow his mother to recover from an illness. Roy's father worked at the stockyards and at other odd jobs to support the family and build up a nest egg while they were there. They spent the next five years in that area before moving back to their homestead.

The Crawfords considered education important, and Roy had started his schooling at the one-room Amherst schoolhouse near the Crawford homestead, but received the next few years of his education in the Kansas City area. He completed his schooling through the eighth grade back at the Amherst schoolhouse. This early exposure to life in a much more densely populated urban area, together with his educational experiences led to a lifelong interest in learning about the extensive world outside his local farming community. He subscribed to, and religiously read, the National Geographic Magazine throughout his adult life, and read numerous other magazines regularly as well.

Albina was quietly competent, efficiently dealing with all of the diverse tasks facing a farm wife of those times. She was an excellent cook, gardener, and homemaker, but she could also handle a team of horses for farm operations when necessary. She was the fourth of ten surviving children in her family, and as was typical for farm children at that time, she shared responsibilities for many household chores including laundry and cooking, and had responsibilities for some of the farm chores. As one of the older children, she also assumed much of the responsibility of caring for some of her younger siblings. She obtained an eighth grade education, split between rural schools in Nebraska and Kansas.

Roy and Albina liked to travel, and after they were married, they made occasional trips. In 1912, they traveled by train to Portland, Oregon to visit Roy's sister Myrtle who lived there at that time. Roy occasionally traveled north in the fall, following the corn harvest where he could earn some extra money, and in 1918 the whole family spent the winter in Rocky Ford, Colorado where Roy found work as a machinist, again to supplement their farm income.

3. The Roy Crawford farmstead in the early 1920s.

The region of Kansas where the Crawfords lived was relatively dry, with an average of about 26 inches of precipitation per year and no well or lake water for irrigation, but Roy developed techniques to maximize his wheat production in this dry area. Because of his success as a farmer, he was able to acquire more land. By 1922, he owned and farmed 640 acres, including the land that his parents had homesteaded. However, life was still difficult in rural Kansas. Even for a successful farmer, there was no electricity, indoor plumbing, or most of the other modern conveniences enjoyed by city dwellers in the 1920s. In the early 1920s, steam-powered threshing machines threshed wheat, but teams of horses still powered other operations on the Crawford farm.

The wheat harvest was the most exciting time on the Crawford farm, a time when there was a flurry of activity to retrieve the grain from the fields. First, the wheat stalks with their heads of grain were cut and bound into bundles. Then the threshing crew would come in with the huge steam-powered threshing machine. The bundles of wheat were fed into the machine and out came the separated wheat grain, then hauled to storage elsewhere on the farm. This activity involved a large crew of men, and created a lot of noise and excitement. Much of the Crawfords' income for the year depended on this wheat crop, so harvest was also a time of stress until all the grain had been successfully harvested and stored.

Because of the importance of harvest, the Crawfords would not leave on their extended western trip until after the 1922 harvest was complete. Albina's younger brother, Bill Hampl, had been helping with the Crawford farming and had agreed to manage the farm and livestock for them while they were gone.

A trip of this magnitude required extensive preparations. The family had been planning for this trip since winter, and Pauline and Clarence were able to remember some of the details—others can only be surmised. Roy bought a Model T Ford truck chassis and had Billy Boxberger, a local carpenter, build a small cabin consisting of a wood floor and a wood frame covered with canvas and painted gray on the back of the truck to make it into an early version of a recreational vehicle. This "RV" would be their home on the trip. This cabin had a window at each side and one at the back, a windshield at the front, and two doors beside the driver and passenger seats. Anyone entering or leaving the RV had to negotiate around one of these seats.

This cabin was definitely not spacious, having an interior space less than half the size of the living room in the Crawford farmhouse.[2] That space had to provide the accommodations for sleeping, cooking, eating, and some of the other daily activities for the four family members. It also had to hold the supplies, clothing, tools, and other equipment needed for their extended trip.

4. Roy, Clarence, Pauline, and Albina wearing their travel clothes and posing in front of the RV.

Inside the RV, they built a bed for Roy and Albina made from an old leather couch that could be folded out and covered with a straw mattress. This couch

---

[2] Estimates made from the Crawfords' pictures, using the known 125-inch wheelbase of the truck as a reference, give the following approximate interior dimensions: cabin width, 5.8 feet; cabin length from rear to windshield, 11.9 feet; height of the cabin, at most 5.2 feet; and door height and width 4.0 feet x 2.0 feet.

doubled as the seat for the kids and possibly for Albina while they were traveling. Pauline and Clarence would sleep in the cabin on another straw mattress. The mattresses would be stored under the bed and could be unrolled at night. They also built in some small cabinets and a space for a folding wood table. They would have their cooking utensils and a two-burner fuel oil (kerosene) stove for cooking.

They needed to take many things with them, so they had to pack efficiently and plan carefully where each item would fit in the RV. The kit containing the cooking and eating utensils demonstrates how compactly some of the items could be packed and stored.

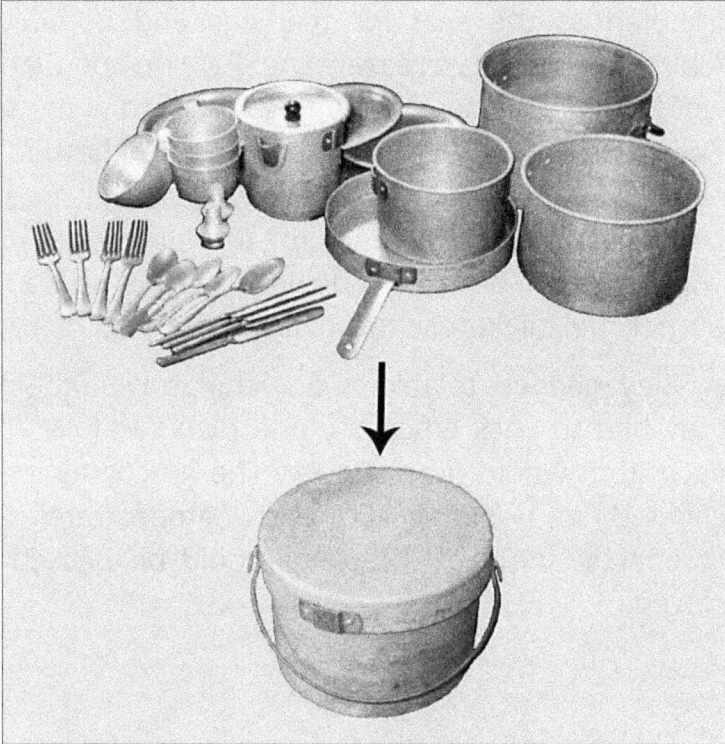

5. The Crawford cooking and eating utensils. All utensils packed inside the largest pot, with the skillet serving as the lid. This pot was 6.5 inches deep and 9.5 inches in diameter.

Albina had been sewing clothes for herself, Pauline, and Clarence to wear on the trip. Men dressed rather formally in those days, and Roy usually wore a white shirt and a necktie for traveling, with the rest of his clothing ranging from bib overalls to a casual jacket and pants or a dress suit. It would be cold in some of the places they were to visit, so they needed to take heavy coats as well. They carefully packed all of this clothing into the limited storage space in the RV.

Clarence and Pauline would miss a year of school. Clarence had attended only one year of school, and the idea of missing the next year was fine with him. Pauline was further advanced in her schooling by this time. She would miss her friends while she was away, so she may have had some misgivings. However, Albina took along books and other materials to give Clarence and Pauline lessons to work on while they were away, so at least they wouldn't be too far behind by the time they got back. Besides, the educational aspects of the trip would more than make up for any missed schooling.

The gas tank of the RV held ten gallons and they could get a little better than ten miles per gallon, so they needed to stop for gasoline every hundred miles or so. There were gas stations along the way, providing gasoline at about 30 cents a gallon, but to be safe, they had to carry extra gas with them in sealed cans in case they couldn't find a gas station when they needed it. They also had to take along a supply of water for the radiator and for cooking and drinking, in case there was none available where they stopped to camp. Gasoline, water, and kerosene for the stove required precious storage space in the RV. The Crawfords anticipated that they would have to make frequent repairs to the RV, so they carried an appropriate selection of tools and spare parts with them as well. A wooden box mounted under the RV cabin provided additional storage space for a few of these items.

Roy had bought a new Kodak camera so they could take pictures of the many sights they would see on the trip. The camera had a special feature—one could lift up a small flap and write a very short label right on the film. Unfortunately, the Crawfords rarely utilized this feature. This camera also had a timer attachment, so it could be set up and then everyone had time to be in place before the camera snapped the group picture. Most of the pictures included in this book were taken with this camera.[3]

6. The No. 1A Autographic Kodak camera
used by the Crawfords on their trip.

[3] This camera took twelve 2 ¼ inch x 4 ¼ inch exposures on one No. A 116 autographic film cartridge.

The Automobile Blue Book (1922 Edition, Volume 4) was their primary travel guide for the trip. That book gave step-by-step directions based on local landmarks for following the main routes between cities and other places of interest in the western half of the United States (other volumes covered the other parts of the U.S.). It also contained information about the quality of the roadways and about interesting features along the way. The book they used is still in the Crawford family, and provided useful details about the routes the Crawfords followed.

7. The Crawford copy of the Automobile Blue Book.

The family had to plan ahead how they would handle the money for gasoline, groceries, and other expenses while on the trip.[4] They probably would not have carried this much cash with them. Most likely, they used traveler's checks. American Express traveler's checks were in use well before this time, and the Crawford

---

[4] The Crawfords' trip is estimated to have cost roughly $1,000 in 1922-1923 dollars for gasoline, groceries, camping fees, film and photo developing, and miscellaneous expenditures during the ten months they were gone. This corresponds to $10,000-$15,000 in 2021 dollars.

family members certainly used them for some of their trips later in life. The bank in Luray at that time was the First National Bank of Luray, and they should have been able to get traveler's checks there.

Before they embarked on their trip, the Crawfords had to decide on a general plan for the route to take. They arranged the route so that they could visit seldom-seen relatives and friends along the way, and that they spend all the winter months in Southern California for Albina's health. Some of the "must-see" places included the Pacific Ocean, Yellowstone, the Grand Canyon, Roosevelt Dam in Arizona, and the Petrified Forest. [5] Some of the articles about the National Parks and about the American Southwest from the National Geographic Magazine may have provided ideas about other areas to visit. In addition, the Automobile Blue Book provided numerous suggestions about sights to see along their route.

Taken together, these sources and conditions provided enough information for the family to develop a general plan for the route and the schedule for this trip. Once underway, they would also make use of local information (newspapers, tourist brochures, etc.) to adjust just where they went and what they saw after they arrived in each place.

---

[5] Completed in 1911, Roosevelt Dam was the world's highest masonry dam, and the resulting Roosevelt Lake was the world's largest artificial lake. Both were sights the Crawfords especially wanted to see.

The Road West: August to November

Crawford Farm near Luray to Denver (~406 miles)[6]

Finally, the decided departure date had arrived, and excitement was in the air. The Crawfords had carefully threshed and stored the wheat crop, had completed their travel preparations, and were ready to leave in early August 1922. Roy would do all the driving on this trip—in fact; Albina never did like to drive an automobile. After a last breakfast at home, they climbed into the RV and headed west. Their first goal was Leoti, a small town in western Kansas, where one of Albina's sisters, Agnes (Hampl) Beach lived with her family.[7] The Model T truck could not travel at more than about 15-20 miles per hour because the transmission was geared to haul heavy loads, so it

---

[6] Mileages cited are based on values given in the *Automobile Blue Book* when available. Otherwise, they are based on the *1927 Rand McNally Road Atlas*.

[7] Map site 1. Map site specifications refer to the route map in figure 1.

took the family most of two days driving in the RV to travel the nearly 200 miles to Leoti.

When they stopped for the night, they had to set up camp. The RV had no electricity, no indoor plumbing, and no refrigerator; but since they didn't have any of those conveniences at home either they didn't really miss them. They did miss the interior space they had at their farmhouse, so they tried to maximize their use of outdoor space or of other campsite facilities whenever possible. They stopped at campgrounds when they were available, but could camp almost anywhere if necessary. Aside from space, the only home convenience that the RV lacked was an outhouse. If their camping spot didn't provide one, a chamber pot or their surroundings had to suffice.

There was a ritual to setting up camp. The stove, cooking utensils, and food had to be unpacked from the RV. The stove would be positioned in a suitable place on the ground, or possibly under a shelter if such were available. Weather permitting, they would set up the folding table outside with some folding chairs, and that was where they would eat their supper and perhaps their breakfast the next morning. If the weather was bad, the table and chairs could be set up in the RV, but this was a tight fit. When it was time to sleep, Roy and Albina folded out their bed in the RV and unrolled a straw mattress onto it. Pauline and Clarence unrolled their straw mattress as well. If the weather permitted they could sleep under the stars, but they could squeeze into the RV to sleep if they had to. Dishes had to be cleaned and everything had to be repacked into the RV before starting out the next day. With minor variations, this process became their ritual nearly every night of the trip.

Along their way they saw some farmers in western Kansas who were still cutting the last of their wheat, using tractor-pulled machines called combines that cut and threshed the wheat in a single operation. The Crawfords had not yet applied this technology on their farm, and Roy stopped to observe and to take some pictures. They marveled at the fact that, unlike on their farm, the land in western Kansas was flat enough to make efficient use of this 36-foot-wide cutter.

8. Harvesting wheat with a combine in western Kansas.

Finally, they arrived at the house where Agnes and Charles Beach and their kids lived. They were tired, but they had made a good start on their great adventure.

9. With the Beach family at Leoti, Kansas. Back: Robert Beach, Agnes Beach, Amy Beach, Howard Beach; Front: Charles Beach holding Ruth Beach, Lorena Beach, Pauline Crawford, Clarence Crawford, Albina Crawford.

They spent a few days with the Beach family and then headed west to Lookout Mountain near Denver, Colorado.[8] It took them two days to get there, plus additional time to make it up Lariat Trail, a 20-foot-wide dirt road with many switchbacks, on the steep east side of the mountain. The Model T truck could make it up grades of as much as 20% so long as the gas tank was at least a quarter full, so that was no

---

[8] Map site 2.

problem. [9] However, the parking brake was not reliable. Whenever they stopped on a grade, Albina jumped out with a small wedge-shaped log they carried for this purpose, and placed the log behind or in front of one of the wheels to keep the truck from rolling down the grade.

When they got to the top of Lookout Mountain, they met Roy's younger brother Charlie Crawford and his wife Minnie, who had driven from their home, which was also near Luray in central Kansas. Charlie and Minnie came in their Model T Ford, prepared for camping with a tent that folded into a box mounted on the side of the car. When they set up their tent, it attached to the car with the car forming one wall of their shelter. Charlie and Minnie continued to accompany Roy, Albina, Pauline, and Clarence for most of the rest of their trip. The Model T could travel almost twice as fast as the RV, so Charlie and Minnie could fit in extra stops or side trips and still catch up with Roy and his family in the RV.

From the top of Lookout Mountain, they could see for miles in several directions. While they were there, they went to see the grave of Buffalo Bill, the star of his famous "Wild West Show."

---

[9] The Model T had no fuel pump, instead using gravity to transfer gasoline from the tank to the carburetor. The level of the gasoline in the tank always had to be higher than the carburetor to provide an uninterrupted supply.

10. Minnie, Charlie, Albina, Clarence, and Roy on Lookout Mountain. Pauline is mostly hidden behind Roy.

Denver to Yellowstone National Park (~674 miles)

A day and a half of easy driving along the National Park-to-Park Highway [10] took them from Lookout Mountain to the farm in Platte County Wyoming where the Bradley Johnson family, formerly from the Luray area, had homesteaded.[11] Bradley was about Roy's age and had grown up near the Crawfords. Bradley and his wife Amelia homesteaded near Glendo in Platte County, Wyoming in 1918. When the Crawford families visited them in 1922, the Johnsons were living in a log cabin on their Wyoming homestead and had two children: Clarence (age 16) and Frances (age 10). The Crawfords spent two or

---

[10] In 1922, most of the roads had names rather than numbers. The modern highway numbering system was not introduced until 1926. By now nearly all of the roads the Crawfords followed have been superseded by numbered interstate highways or else by other major numbered U.S. or state highways, most of which are paved and have multiple lanes with traffic moving at 70 miles per hour or more in many places.

[11] Map site 3.

three days there, and Pauline and Clarence spent part of that time riding on the Johnson horses.

11. Bradley Johnson's farm in Wyoming. From left: Bradley Johnson, Clarence Johnson, Frances Johnson, Amelia Johnson, Clarence Crawford, Albina Crawford, Pauline Crawford, Roy Crawford, Charlie Crawford, and Minnie Crawford.

12. Frances Johnson, Pauline, and Clarence Crawford in front of the RV at Bradley Johnson's farm.

13. Clarence Crawford playing cowboy at Bradley Johnson's farm.

After their visit at the Bradley Johnson farm, the travelers followed the National Park-to-Park Highway (also called the Yellowstone Highway along this stretch) northwest to Thermopolis.[12] This part of the trip was challenging because there wasn't a well-defined road here. Instead, there was about a half-mile wide swath of ruts where previous travelers had made their own way across the hills. Travelers picked out one set of ruts to follow, and if that wasn't satisfactory, they just moved over to a different set.

> "The roads are dirt practically the entire distance and are bad in wet or extremely dry weather. . . The worst stretch is usually

_____

[12] Map site 4.

between Caspar and Thermopolis, this often being very badly worn and rutted on account of the heavy travel through the oil fields." — Automobile Blue Book, p. 582.

"The road winds over hills and valleys through a sparsely settled, barren sagebrush country." —Automobile Blue Book, p. 585.

It was nearly 260 miles from the Bradley Johnson place to Thermopolis, and this section of the trip required several days of driving.

The large hot springs near Thermopolis in Hot Springs County, Wyoming contain mineral-laden waters heated by geothermal processes. These springs were sacred to the Shoshone people living in the area, but by the late 1800s, squatters had already settled on much of the Shoshone Reservation area surrounding the springs. To compensate the Shoshones, in 1897 the U.S. Government purchased 100 square miles of Shoshone Reservation land that included the springs, and then gave the square mile containing the springs to the state of Wyoming. As part of this arrangement, the springs were and still are open to the public free of charge.

The railroad reached Thermopolis in 1910, but before that, the area was so isolated that it became a popular hideout for notorious outlaws including Butch Cassidy and the Sundance Kid. The railroad opened Thermopolis to visitors desiring to bathe in the geothermally heated waters containing minerals considered good for one's health, and to view the variety of peculiar formations created from minerals deposited by these springs. The population of Thermopolis had reached about 2,000 by the time the Crawfords were there.

14. Big Horn Spring, Thermopolis, Wyoming

15. Charlie, Minnie, Pauline, Clarence, and Albina in front of a mineral deposit at Thermopolis.

The travelers enjoyed the sights at Thermopolis, and then continued along the National Park-to-Park Highway to Shoshone

Canyon[13] near Cody, Wyoming. It took about half a day to get there. Shoshone Canyon is a deep narrow gorge cut by the Shoshone River as it flows eastward from Yellowstone Park through the Rattlesnake Mountains. Shoshone Dam across this canyon was completed in 1910, forming Shoshone Lake.[14] Roy took pictures of the canyon right below the lake, and then they traveled into the portion of the canyon above the lake. That route followed the bottom of the canyon beside the river and led right into Yellowstone Park, about 50 miles from the lake.

However, this section of the trip proved to hold several challenges. In many places, the walls of the canyon were nearly vertical. The road through Shoshone Canyon was only one lane wide, with wider spots every half-mile or so where vehicles could pull over when meeting oncoming traffic. Sometimes a vehicle would have to back up to the nearest wide spot to allow an oncoming vehicle to pass. Because the canyon was so narrow, the engineers had found it necessary to tunnel through the granite walls in places to provide a path for the road.

The cabin of the RV had been built with a rounded top, but at the first tunnel they came to the rounded

---

[13] Map site 5.

[14] The lake and dam are different now. In 1946 Shoshone Dam was renamed Buffalo Bill Dam. In 1985, the dam was renovated, raising the top by 25 feet and extending the lake further upstream.

cabin did not fit the rounded opening of the tunnel. The RV could not pass through. After a few choice words from Roy, they backed off to a place to camp, and spent several days rebuilding the cabin with a new rounded top carefully designed to fit through the tunnels. The cabin remained in that new shape for the rest of the trip. Charlie and Minnie's Model T was much smaller and needed no modifications. Charlie took pictures after everyone finally made it through the first tunnel.[15]

16. Shoshone Canyon, just downstream from Shoshone Dam.

---

[15] In 1960, the Shoshone Canyon road was moved further from the river and was made into a modern highway with new tunnels, bearing little resemblance to the road and tunnels the Crawfords encountered.

17. Road and tunnel beside the river in Shoshone Canyon

18. Albina, Clarence, Roy, and Pauline with the RV in the tunnel on the Shoshone Canyon road.

19. Minnie with their car in the tunnel.

After finally making it through the tunnel, they followed the Shoshone Canyon road into Yellowstone Park.[16] They spent nearly two weeks there because there were so many remarkable sights to see and so many good places to fish. (Roy loved to fish, and they all enjoyed eating the fish.)

Yellowstone National Park was the first National Park in the U.S., created by act of Congress in 1872. It is primarily in Wyoming, but it extends into Idaho and Montana as well. Woodrow Wilson signed the bill creating the National Park Service in 1916, and the Park Service took over administration of the park in 1917. Prior to this, the U.S. Army managed the park and built Fort Yellowstone there. The average

---

[16] Map site 6.

elevation of Yellowstone Park is about 8,000 feet above sea level. The Crawfords needed time to get accustomed to activities at this altitude, and they were frequently out of breath there.

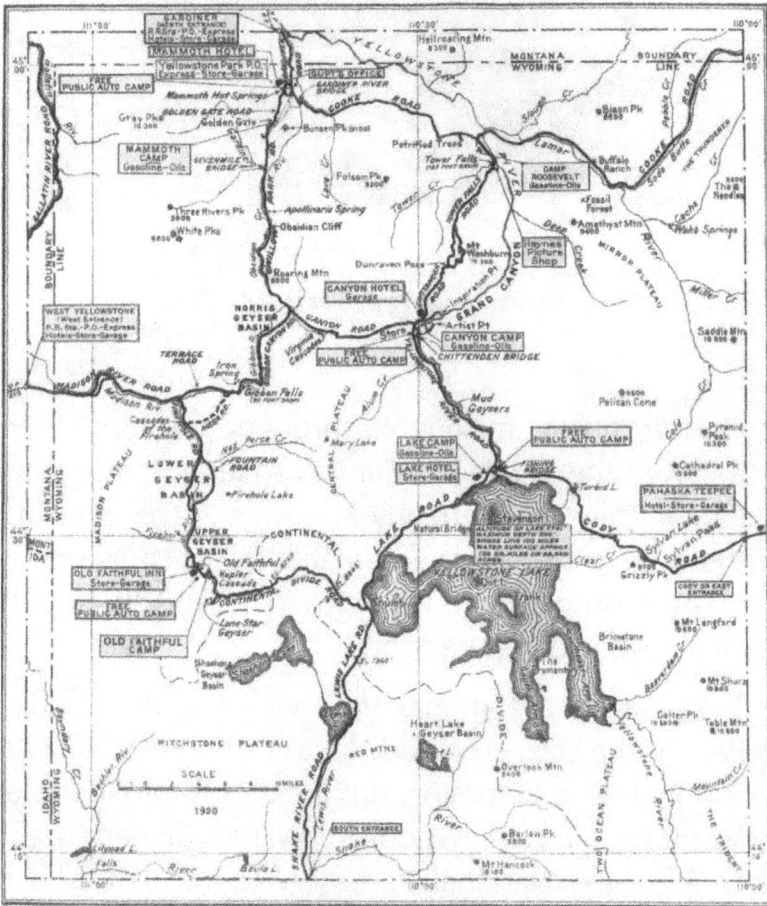

MAP OF YELLOWSTONE NATIONAL PARK

20. 1920 Map of Yellowstone National Park.

By 1922, Yellowstone Park was hosting about 100,000 visitors per year. This was a significant increase over earlier years, but at any given time, there were still at most a few thousand visitors in the entire 3,500 square miles spanned by the park.[17] The park was also becoming well equipped to handle the visitors. There was a system of roads providing easy access to most of the major attractions, although most of the roads looping around within the park were one-way due to the "high volume" of traffic. The Park was configured to accommodate tourists. It had several appealing auto campgrounds with showers, a store where they could buy groceries, and gas stations where they could get gas or repairs for their vehicles. Speed limits in the Park were 10-12 miles per hour on the grades and up to 25 miles per hour on the level straight sections. The park facilities would close for the winter on September 20, but the Crawfords had arrived there in early September, leaving them enough time to spend in the park while the services were still open.

Of course, they took many pictures in Yellowstone. A remarkable aspect of these pictures, at least by today's standards, is how few Park visitors are seen in

---

[17] The kind of unhurried and uncrowded visit enjoyed by the Crawfords is no longer possible. The annual number of visitors to Yellowstone National Park has increased 35-fold, from about 100,000 in 1922 to about 3,500,000 in 2010.

them. The Crawfords definitely did not have to compete with crowds to see the sights at the Park.

Left: 21. Albina, Pauline, Roy, and Clarence entering Yellowstone Park at the East Entrance.

Below: 22. The RV on Sylvan Pass Road in Yellowstone Park near the East Entrance. Two cars are stopped there as well—the one people are standing around is Charlie and Minnie's.

Yellowstone is noted for its many geysers, some of which are spectacular. The National Park Service's 1920 brochure for motorists to Yellowstone National Park included a section devoted to describing the points of interest in the park. There the Park Service waxed lyrical about the geysers, calling them all out by name and ascribing human-like personalities to some of them. Descriptive names like Constant, Whirligig, Valentine, Black Growler, Minute Man, Fearless, Vixen, Spasmodic, and Young Hopeful provide clues to the personalities to be expected from the individual geysers.

The three geysers that the Crawfords managed to photograph in the act of erupting were all in the Upper Geyser Basin. Of the Grotto Geyser, the brochure stated, "The empty crater is more interesting than the eruption." The Giant Geyser was said to be "the greatest geyser of them all, but rather uncertain in its periods", and Old Faithful was described as "the tourist's friend . . . it plays often and with regularity." They did not get a picture of a nearby geyser, the Giantess, a large and powerful but irregular geyser, perhaps because the brochure warned, "It is just as well not to approach the Giantess too close. It has not much consideration for the safety of its visitors and has been known to break forth into eruption with no warning whatever from its quiet, smiling crater."[18]

---

[18] *Yellowstone NP: Rules and Regulations,* 1920.

23. Grotto Geyser in Yellowstone Park

24. Old Faithful Geyser.

25. Giant Geyser.

The loop road through the Park crosses the Continental Divide at Craig Pass (one of several crossings within the park), about eight miles down the road from Old Faithful. The Crawfords stopped there next to Isa Lake. The waters from this lake "hesitate whether to flow out one end into Pacific waters or out the other into Atlantic waters and usually compromise by going both directions."[19]

26. The Crawford families at the Continental Divide in Yellowstone Park. All got out of their vehicles to appreciate the occasion.

27. Lower Yellowstone Falls near Canyon Camp.

---

[19] Yellowstone NP: Rules and Regulations, 1920.

28. *Grand Canyon of the Yellowstone River near Canyon Camp.*

29. *Dragon's Mouth Springs near the Mud Geysers*

30. Albina and Minnie posing on Fishing Cone at the edge of the "Thumb" of Yellowstone Lake.

31. Yellowstone Lake.

32. Buffalo herd at the Buffalo Ranch in Yellowstone Park. The RV and the Crawford families are on the far side of the herd.

33. Bear in Yellowstone Park. The item in its mouth may be a food wrapper obtained from a visitor's campsite.

34. Mule deer in Yellowstone Park

35. Roy with trout he caught in Yellowstone Park.

Yellowstone National Park to Portland (~962 miles)

The road out of the southern entrance to Yellowstone Park led directly to Jackson Lake and the Teton Mountains,[20] a few miles south of Yellowstone Park. The Teton Range is the youngest mountain range in the Rocky Mountains. In addition to 13,775-foot-high Grand Teton, there are another nine peaks in the Teton Range rising to over 12,000 feet. Jackson Lake, originally a natural lake, is situated in a valley in Teton County, Wyoming, between the Teton Mountains to the West and the Yellowstone Plateau to the north. Jackson Lake Dam, first built in 1911 and enlarged in 1916, added 33 feet of depth to the lake to provide water for farmers in Idaho to use for irrigation. Access to this valley is so steep that the area is usually referred to as Jackson Hole.

The Crawfords didn't stay long at Jackson Lake, but they were there long enough for Roy to take pictures of Jackson Lake and the Teton Mountains and of

---

[20] Map site 7.

Jackson Lake Dam.[21] Big dams were not to be found in Kansas, so the family made special efforts to visit a number of them during this trip.

36. Teton Mountains and Jackson Lake, Wyoming.

---

[21] This region has become a major tourist destination since the Crawfords were there. Grand Teton National Park was created in 1929 to protect the major peaks in the Teton Range, and the valley of Jackson Hole was added to this Park in 1950. Approximately 2,750,000 people visited Grand Teton National Park in 2010.

37. Jackson Lake Dam, Wyoming.

From Jackson Lake, the travelers crossed into Idaho and followed the Snake River to Pocatello, Idaho. Beginning at Pocatello, they took the Old Oregon Trail, which mostly followed the Snake River, to the Oregon border. In Oregon, they continued on the Old Oregon Trail until they reached Pendleton, Oregon on the Columbia Plateau.[22] The Columbia Plateau in Eastern Oregon had conditions that were ideal for dryland wheat farming (wheat grown on unirrigated land in a relatively low-rainfall zone, the kind of conditions experienced on the Crawford farm), and it was the primary source of wheat in Oregon. Because it was further north, the harvest there occurred much later than harvest in Kansas and the threshing was still in progress. The Crawfords encountered some farmers threshing wheat similarly

---

[22] Map site 8.

to the way it was done on the Crawford farm. Naturally, they had to stop for a bit to watch this operation.

38. Men, horses, engines, and machinery involved in threshing wheat on the Columbia Plateau in Oregon.

39. Oregon farmers threshing wheat.

Their route beyond Pendleton took them onto the recently completed Historic Columbia River Highway,[23]

---

[23] Map site 9.

the first planned scenic roadway in the United States. It was built between 1913 and 1922 and stretched along the Oregon side of the Columbia River.[24] A novel feature was that this highway was paved over its entire length, the first such road they had encountered. The Crawfords took pictures of several of the sights along this highway.

40. The Crawford families enjoying the view of the Columbia River.

One of the first sights the travelers encountered, Shepperds Dell Bridge was the second bridge built on the Columbia River Highway. Completed in 1914, the graceful bridge spanned Young's Creek in Multnomah County, Oregon.

---

[24] Columbia River Highway No. 2 (later Interstate 84) was built in the 1930s to permit through traffic to bypass the Historic Columbia River Highway, but the old two-lane road remains as a scenic route along the river.

41. The Crawfords on the Shepperds Dell Bridge.

The Crawfords found the Cascade Locks quite impressive, and spent some time exploring them. Early travelers on the Columbia River were forced to portage around the impassable rapids of the Columbia River Cascades. In 1878, a set of locks were completed allowing riverboats to travel much farther up the river from Portland. These impressive Cascade Locks were used for more than 50 years until the Bonneville Dam was built.[25]

---

[25] The Cascade Locks can no longer be seen. The Bonneville Dam, completed in 1938, created a lake that inundated the Cascade Locks, and they remain buried beneath the waters.

42. Cascade Locks on the Columbia River.

Another natural stopping point was Vista House located at Crown Point in Multnomah County, Oregon, 733 feet above the Columbia River. Vista House was completed in 1918 and was intended as "an observatory from which the view both up and down the Columbia could be viewed in silent communion with the infinite."[26] It also served as a memorial to Oregon pioneers and as a comfort station to travelers along the Historic Columbia River Highway. Its marble interior and brass fixtures led some Oregonians to

---

[26] *"The Vista House Story"* (http://vistahouse.com/history/the-vista-house-story/). Friends of Vista House.

refer to it as "the $100,000 outhouse"[27] when it was first built. The top of Vista House is accessible by stairs, and from there one can look to the west to see Portland on the Oregon side of the river and Vancouver on the Washington side. The view to the east includes Beacon Rock on the Washington side of the gorge.

43. The Crawfords posing in front of Vista House.

The Columbia River Highway led the Crawfords into Portland,[28] the largest city in Oregon, and a major port at the confluence of the Willamette and Columbia Rivers. Pioneer settlers began arriving in large

---

[27] *Dedication ceremony for Vista House, Crown Point, Oregon, ca. 1919*
(http://content.lib.washington.edu/cdm4/item_viewer.php?CISOR OOT=/alaskawcanada&CISOPTR=1803). University of Washington Libraries.

[28] Map site 10.

numbers in the fertile Willamette Valley via the Oregon Trail in the 1830s. Portland was founded around 1850 and by 1920, it had a population of about 260,000.[29]

Roy's sister Myrtle (Crawford) Thomas and her husband Ralph Thomas had migrated from Kansas to a farm near Portland, Oregon in about 1905. By 1917, Ralph was working for the railroad and they had moved into Portland. The Crawfords spent some time with them in Portland. Ralph's father and two of his brothers were also there, so there was a good old-fashioned family get-together with much reminiscing about earlier times.

44. Front row: Clarence Crawford, Myrtle Thomas, Pauline Crawford, Albina Crawford, Minnie Crawford. Back row: Ralph's older brother Curtis, Ralph Thomas, Ralph's father Aaron, Ralph's younger brother Guy, Charlie Crawford.

---

[29] At the time of this writing, the last census data available was for 2010. The population of Portland was about 580,000 in 2010.

The Willamette River empties into the Columbia River in Portland. A set of falls on the Willamette about 20 miles south of Portland initially precluded shipping by river boats from further up the river directly to Portland and beyond. The Willamette Falls Locks, completed around the falls in 1873, turned the Willamette River into a major artery, allowing shipping by steamboat from the Willamette Valley to Portland and thence to overseas markets. The near boat in Fig. 45 is a stern-wheel steamboat (probably a passenger boat or ferry). Side-wheel and stern-wheel paddle-wheel boats were commonly used for river traffic because they could travel in relatively shallow water.

45. Paddle-wheel steamboat on the Willamette River in Portland.

While the Crawfords were in Portland, they visited some of the nearby sights. They took a paddle-wheel steamboat trip up the Willamette and the Yamhill Rivers, passing through the locks at Lafayette on the Yamhill River before returning to Portland.[30]

46. Postcard from the Yamhill River locks.

---

[30] The Yamhill Locks continued in use until the 1950s. The dam for these locks was later destroyed with explosives to facilitate the use of the river by spawning salmon. However, the lock walls and the lock keeper's residence remain.

Portland to San Francisco
(~741 miles)

The route along the Oregon coast, which later became U.S. Route 101, was under construction during the 1920s. Since much of it was incomplete in 1922, the Crawfords instead followed the Pacific Highway south from Portland. The Pacific Highway (not to be confused with the Pacific Coast Highway) auto trail was built in the 1910s and 1920s by the states of Washington, Oregon, and California. From Vancouver, Washington to Sacramento, California, the Pacific Highway followed the track of the Siskiyou Trail, based on an ancient network of Native American footpaths connecting the Pacific Northwest with the Central Valley of California. From Portland, the Pacific Highway ran through the Willamette Valley to southern Oregon. It then made its way through a mountainous region, passing near Mount Shasta in California before reaching the California Central Valley, which it followed to near Sacramento before veering toward San Francisco. The Oregon section of the Pacific Highway, completely paved by 1923 from border-to-border, became the first border-to-border paved highway west of the Mississippi.

The Willamette River Valley extends almost straight south from Portland for more than 100 miles, to just past Cottage Grove, Oregon. It is an extremely productive farming region where a wide variety of plants and animals are grown. Of course, the Crawfords had to stop and inspect some of these farming operations.

Hazelnuts, walnuts, and chestnuts were important crops in Oregon. The Crawfords stopped to watch some of the nuts being harvested, a labor-intensive operation. First, a canvas was spread on the ground under the tree. Then one or more persons on the ground used sticks to knock the nuts loose from the lower branches, while another person climbed the tree to shake the higher branches. The nuts fell from the tree onto the canvas, where they could be easily collected and transferred to a basket or other container. When all the nuts that were ready to harvest were collected from that tree, the operation was moved to another tree and repeated.

The Crawfords also visited a large turkey farm. Oregon was once one of the leaders in introducing modern turkey farming to America. In the 1920s and 1930s, turkey production in Oregon grew significantly, and at one time Oregon produced 30% of the west coast supply of turkey.

After leaving the Willamette valley, their road followed the Rogue River valley across the scenic Siskiyou Mountains to the California border. Just beyond the border, they crossed the Klamath River near Hornbrook, California.[31] There the Crawfords visited a wooden weir where men from the state fishery service were trapping adult salmon as part of a salmon propagation project. To propagate salmon artificially, the eggs and sperm first had to be harvested from live fish. A wooden weir, constructed across a stream, impeded the upstream migration of spawning adults. An opening in the weir led the salmon into a cage where they waited until their sperm and eggs were physically removed by the hatchery staff. These "harvested" fish were then typically discarded, and their eggs and sperm were transported to a hatchery where workers would manually fertilize the eggs and rear the young fish until their release back into the river system.

The workers at the weir gave the Crawfords a couple of these salmon that would otherwise have been discarded. The families had great fun posing with the fish and their fishing poles, pretending that they actually caught these salmon, and then enjoyed themselves even more as the fish became a delicious evening meal.

---

[31] Map site 11.

47. Weir to trap salmon.

48. Minnie, Pauline, Clarence, Albina, and Charlie by the RV
with the two salmon given to them at the weir.

49. Minnie, Charlie, and Albina with the larger of the salmon.

50. Roy posing with the salmon, holding a fishing pole, and grinning as though he had caught these fish.

The Crawfords continued south on the Pacific Highway through the Klamath and Shasta River canyons in Northern California, passing within a few miles of Mount Shasta on their way to the Sacramento Valley. However, the only photo of Mount Shasta found in the Crawford trip album was a severely overexposed picture taken from much farther away. (Painstaking reconstruction managed to extract Figure 51 from a portion of this overexposed picture.) It seems extremely likely that they would have taken additional pictures of such an imposing sight as they passed closer to it. The absence of any other Mount Shasta pictures suggests that the family may have managed to spoil most of the roll of film they were using at the time.

51. Mount Shasta from a distance, as seen through the RV window on the Pacific Highway in the Sacramento Valley.

The first extensive and successful development of irrigation in the Sacramento Valley occurred in the early 1900s. By the end of the 1920s, fifty-one irrigation systems delivered water to 282,000 acres. In the 1920s, only a few farmers with large farms owned tractors, so teams of horses were still used to dig many of the ditches for irrigation and/or drainage.

52. Men working with teams of horses to dig irrigation ditches in Northern California.

The fine-wine industry in California got its start in Sonoma County in the mid-1800s. By 1900, many California wines were receiving medals in European competitions and America had a well-developed commercial wine producing business. However, in 1920, the Volstead act and the Eighteenth Amendment to the U.S. Constitution forbade the "manufacture, sale, or transportation of intoxicating liquors," and this largely destroyed the American wine industry. Although some wineries managed to survive by obtaining permits to make wines used for medicinal, sacramental and non-beverage additive purposes, production dropped 94% from 1919 to 1925. Some vineyards also sold their grapes as table grapes. By 1922, many of the vineyards were no longer in production, but most of the old vines had not yet been ripped out.

53. Old grape vines no longer in production in Northern California.

In early October the Crawfords passed by Sacramento and headed out of the valley to San Francisco,[32] which they reached by taking a ferry across the upper San Francisco Bay (ferries from Oakland or from Sausalito were the two options in 1922). The 1848 California gold rush started a boom in population of the San Francisco area, and by 1852 San Francisco had a population of about 35,000, rising to about 230,000 by 1880. The massive earthquake of

---

[32] Map site 12

1906 destroyed nearly 80% of the city, including almost the entire downtown core. San Franciscans had almost completely rebuilt the city by 1920, and by then the population had increased to 500,000.[33]

The Crawford families didn't spend much time in the city itself, but San Francisco gave them their first glimpse of the Pacific Ocean. There they saw the shipwrecked tanker Lyman Stewart, which had wrecked near Lands End in San Francisco shortly before they arrived. The Lyman Stewart was a tanker built by the Union Iron Works in San Francisco for the Union Oil Company. On October 7, 1922, the Lyman Stewart was sailing through the Golden Gate when the freighter Walter A. Luchenbach rammed her. The Lyman Stewart immediately began to sink and the crew abandoned ship, but the Captain stayed aboard to drive the ship onto the rocks to prevent her from sinking to the bottom. There were no casualties, most of the oil was retrieved from the tanker, and the Lyman Stewart was abandoned where she lay. This wreck was within yards of the end of a popular streetcar line (No. 1 Sutter and California line, "the Cliff Line"), and so drew huge crowds.

---

[33] The population of San Francisco was about 800,000 in 2010.

54. The wreck of the Lyman Stewart at Lands End in San Francisco

55. The Golden Gate, with the wreck of the Lyman Stewart in the foreground.[34]

---

[34] This view is now dominated by the Golden Gate Bridge, which was begun in 1933 and completed in 1937, spanning the passage shown at the right.

The Taiyo Maru arrived in San Francisco on October 8, 1922. Fortuitously, this was while the Crawfords were there, so they were able to watch her dock. Ships were a novelty for the farmers from Kansas, and the Crawfords found them fascinating. They were able to observe and photograph many ships of different types during the course of this trip.

56. Taiyo Maru in San Francisco.

The Taiyo Maru was a palatial liner of the Oriental Steamship Company, Toyo Kisen Kaisha, and was the largest passenger vessel on the Pacific Ocean at the time. She was originally the Cap Finisterre, a passenger ship built by the Germans shortly before the outbreak of World War I. After the war, she was allocated to the Japanese government as part of the war reparations. She went into service between Japan and North America in 1921, and could carry 1,468 passengers.[35]

57. Posing at the Sunol Water Temple in Sunol, California.

---

[35] The Taiyo Maru continued to carry passengers across the Pacific until October 1941. On her last trip from Yokohama to Honolulu, she included three Japanese Imperial Navy officers in disguise among her crew. The three Japanese officers reconnoitered the entrance to Pearl Harbor while they were there, and when they returned to Yokohama these officers provided information for the midget submarines that were part of the Pearl Harbor attack. An American submarine sank the Taiyo Maru as she transported ammunition in May 1942.

On their way out of the area, the Crawfords took a side trip to the Sunol Water Temple located at Sunol in Alameda County to the east of San Francisco Bay. This "Temple" covers a white-tiled cistern where water from the Pleasanton well fields and Arroyo de la Laguna flow into a deeper channel to the Niles Aqueduct and across San Francisco Bay. The Spring Valley Water Company, which had a monopoly on water service to San Francisco, completed the Temple in 1910. The Temple, modeled after the Temple of Vesta in Tivoli, Italy, was built in an area by itself, away from the city, and it looked strangely out of place standing alone out there.

They also took a side trip to Big Basin Redwoods State Park, the first state park created in California. This park had a large stand of ancient coastal redwoods, numerous waterfalls, varied environments, and abundant animal and bird life. In addition, it had cabins to rent, a restaurant, general store, barbershop, gas station, and a photographic studio. Campsites cost 50 cents a night.

58. Post card from Big Basin Redwoods State Park. "Giant Tree, Big Tree Grove, Santa Cruz, California, 306 Ft. High, 65 Ft. in Circumference, Estimated 5000 Years Old."

San Francisco to Los Angeles (~445 miles)

The travelers proceeded southward through Santa Cruz to Salinas where they joined El Camino Real, a road that approximately followed an early Spanish footpath linking the forts, towns, and religious missions that Spain had built throughout southern California. This trail provided local transportation links between colonial settlements but most goods and passengers moved by ships over the long distances up and down the coast. By the late nineteenth century, the route as a whole had faded into obscurity, although some local segments of the old trail were still heavily used.

The rise of the automobile early in the twentieth century led to demand for a well-maintained state highway. At the same time, regional boosters began to tout California's missions as sites where tourists could commune with the romantic past. To provide a pseudo-historical basis for El Camino Real, they invented sentimental stories about Franciscan fathers traveling along the road from mission to mission, which were supposedly spaced one day apart along the trail. The 1910 State Highways Act authorized construction of a paved road along the route of El Camino Real. However, construction of the paved road proceeded slowly and for many years, much of the historic road remained a primitive trail with streams to ford and steep hills to climb. Occasionally, automobiles trapped in the mud required rescue by teams of horses. This was probably still the condition of some parts of the road at the time of the Crawfords' trip, but they managed the route without being stuck. Much of this road became U.S. Highway 101 in 1925, shortly after this highway construction project was complete.

El Camino Real ran more-or-less parallel to the coast, separated from the Pacific Ocean by mountain ranges. However, it cut over to run along the coast for a short stretch near San Luis Obispo, and then again starting near the Santa Ynez Mountains and continuing through Santa Barbara and on to Los Angeles. The Crawfords drove through lightly populated ranch land along much of the way, seeing only an occasional house. It may have been scenic along much of El Camino, but they didn't take many pictures on this stretch. They did stop at Santa Barbara[36] to spend time on the beach there, however.

---

[36] Map site 13

59. Isolated stone house along El Camino Real.

Santa Barbara lies between the steeply rising Santa Ynez Mountains and the Pacific Ocean along a south-facing section of coastline about 80 miles west-northwest of Los Angeles. In 1922, its population was about 20,000 and growing, its growth fueled in part by the arrival of the railroad around 1900 and by the discovery of offshore oil.

60. Crawfords on Thousand Steps Beach at Santa Barbara.

Winter in

Southern

California

November to January: The Los Angeles Area

The Crawfords got to Los Angeles[37] in early November, having traveled about 3,200 miles, not counting side trips, and they remained in that general area until early January. To Kansans, the weather there felt positively balmy for that time of year (60s and 70s in the daytime), and there was an abundance of sights to see and things to do in and near Los Angeles. The Crawfords also spent some time in nearby Pasadena, Riverside, San Bernardino, and Palm Springs.

Founded on September 4, 1781, Los Angeles grew as a frontier outpost as soldiers and other settlers came into town and stayed. By 1821, Los Angeles had grown into the largest self-sustaining farming community in Southern California. California joined the U.S. in 1848, shortly before the discovery of gold in that state. During the gold rush years, Los Angeles supplied beef and other foodstuffs to the hungry

---

[37] Map site 14.

miners in the north, leading to its title as the "Queen of the Cow Counties." By 1900, Los Angeles had become a major city with port and railway facilities, banks, and factories and its population had risen to 100,000. With the discovery of oil there in 1892, the Los Angeles area was soon producing one-quarter of the world's total supply. By 1922, the population of Los Angeles had reached more than 600,000, and the emergent oil industry along with the world-leading Hollywood film industry pointed toward a booming economy and a rapidly expanding real estate industry.[38]

The San Pedro Harbor in Los Angeles was the home port for most of the big Navy ships in the Pacific Fleet. The Crawfords were able to tour the battleship Nevada there.[39] They must have known someone in the Navy, because they had an escorted tour of the ship while there was hardly anyone else on it.

---

[38] The population of Los Angeles was about 3,800,000 in 2010, six times what it was when the Crawfords were there.

[39] The battleship Nevada was ordered in 1911 and was active in the Atlantic Ocean before and during World War I. She transferred to the Pacific in 1919. From 1919 to 1940, San Pedro harbor in Los Angeles was her home port. The Nevada remained active until after World War II. After being damaged during the attack on Pearl Harbor in 1941, the USS Nevada beached herself to prevent blocking the harbor entrance. She was later salvaged, modernized, and provided support during the D-Day landing in Europe. She was considered too old to be kept in service after World War II and was used for target practice.

*61. Pauline, Clarence, Albina, Minnie,
unknown naval officer and Charlie on the
battleship Nevada in San Pedro harbor.*

Roy went to see the automobile races at the Beverly Hills Speedway, a 1.25-mile circumference wooden board track in Beverly Hills, California. Built for automobile racing in 1919, the Speedway occupied 275 acres and hosted its first race in February 1920. The track was the first in the United States built with banked turns, and racers reached speeds over 100 miles per hour there. The speedway operated for four years and attracted many well-known racers.[40]

62. A large crowd in the grandstand and infield at the Beverly Hills Speedway.

63. The parking lot at the Beverly Hills Speedway was full of cars—a very popular place.

---

[40] The Speedway was one of the premier race tracks in the world, but because of rapidly increasing real estate values, the Speedway became an uneconomical use of the land it occupied; in 1924, after only four years of operation, the Speedway was shut down and racing activities were moved a few miles away to Culver City. By 1928, the Beverly Wilshire Hotel occupied part of the site previously occupied by the Speedway.

On one excursion, the Crawfords set out for Santa Monica Pier—two adjoining piers originally owned by separate owners. The long narrow Municipal Pier, which had no amenities, opened in 1909 to carry sewer pipes beyond the breakers, so the sewage dumping into the bay would no longer wash back onto the shore. It was successful, allowing Charles Looff and his son to build the short wide Pleasure Pier to the south in 1916 in an area now free of sewage. The Crawfords spent some time at the Pleasure Pier. What a place! Attractions included the Looff Hippodrome building that contained several different carousels and other attractions, the Blue Streak Racer wooden roller coaster, a bowling and billiards parlor, and a fun house. They also spent some time on the beach, which was right by the pier. Moreover, when they turned and looked the other way they could see the Santa Monica mountains right behind them.

64. The Pleasure Pier at Santa Monica.

65. The Blue Streak Racer roller coaster at the Pleasure Pier.

66. Santa Monica Bay with the Santa Monica Mountains in the background.

Los Angeles and automobiles seemed to be made for each other. Everywhere the travelers went there were places one could drive up and buy something to eat or drink. Often the buildings were uniquely shaped to advertise their wares; Los Angeles was noted for this style known as programmatic architecture. An example is the Barrel Inn establishment selling everything from cigars to cider and candy.

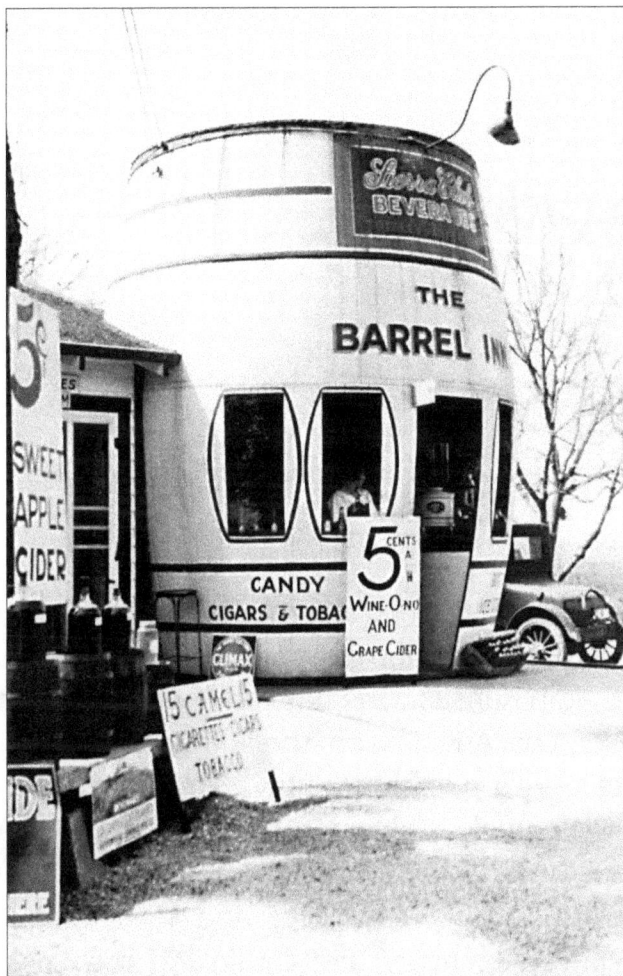

67. Barrel-shaped roadside stand in Los Angeles.

Some residential areas in Los Angeles had gracious tree-lined avenues for the automobiles.

68. Wide, tree-lined residential street with electric streetlights in the Los Angeles area.

Roy loved to drive on mountain roads with steep hills and curves; perhaps because there was nothing like that in Kansas. One day they headed out the north side of Los Angeles on the Ridge Route. The Ridge Route was a two-lane highway between Los Angeles and Bakersfield, California. It opened in 1915 and was paved with a 20-foot-wide 4-inch-thick reinforced concrete pad between 1917 and 1921, making it the first paved highway directly linking the Los Angeles Basin with the San Joaquin Valley. It ran over the Tejon Pass and the rugged Sierra Pelona Mountains. Historical landmarks along the Route included the National Forest Inn, Reservoir Summit, Kelly's Half Way Inn, Tumble Inn, and Sandberg's Summit Hotel.

The Ridge Route had 7% grades in several places, and the speed limit of 15 miles per hour was enforced over much of the route, making the trip from Los Angeles to Bakersfield (about 112 miles on today's roads) take about 12 hours. The Ridge Route had so many sharp curves that it was said to be equivalent to going around 110 complete circles.[41]

Because many early cars and trucks had no fuel pumps, it was common to see vehicles going backwards up the steep grades. An early truck driver on the Route said, "In the 20s and 30s, not too many trucks had air brakes, they were mostly mechanical brakes. You had to be very careful. You went up slow, and you came down slow. The saviors for many on the Old Ridge Road were the banks (sides of hills). If you began to see your brakes burning, you headed for the banks, and you'd 'bank' her."[42]

---

[41] It is no longer possible to experience driving on the "Ridge Route." This road was bypassed in 1933-34 by the three-lane U.S. Route 99, which could handle increased traffic and eliminated many curves. Interstate 5 replaced U.S. Route 99 around 1968. The portion of the Ridge Route within Angeles National Forest was added to the National Register of Historic Places in 1997. Much of the original Ridge Route has been closed, but some remnants of the road continue to be used by local traffic.

[42] *Ridge Route history: The long and winding road*, Andy Kehe, The Bakersfield Californian, Sep 26, 2015.

69. Serpentine Drive on the Ridge Route between Castaic and Tejon Pass, near Los Angeles.

70. Albina, Pauline, and Clarence with the RV at the Newhall Tunnel on the Ridge Route.

71. Pauline, Albina, and Clarence with the RV, Charlie and Minnie's car behind them, and another RV following, near Granite Gate on the Ridge Route.

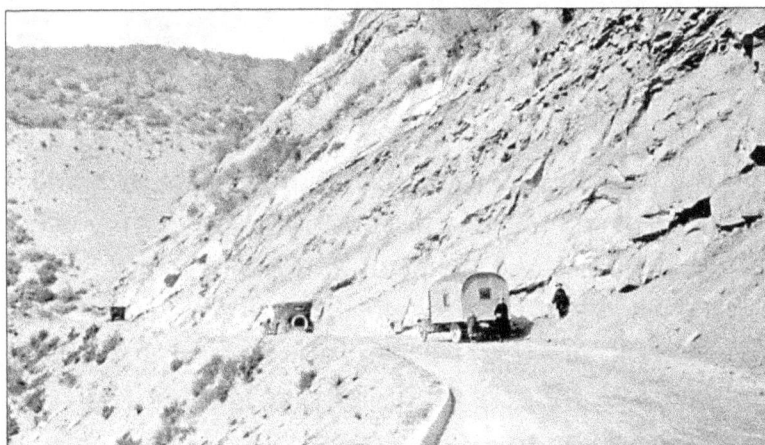

72. The Crawford vehicles stopped near Sandberg's View on the Ridge Route.

73. The RV near Sandberg's View on the Ridge Route.

74. The Grapevine portion of the Ridge Route.

The Crawfords probably didn't make the full 12-hour trip to Bakersfield. More likely, they turned around after the Grapevine and headed back over the Ridge Route to Los Angeles. In any case, the pictures they took on this trip enable one to imagine the curves, switchbacks, and steep grades in the road—a little like riding the roller coaster!

Near Sylmar at the Los Angeles end of the Ridge Route, they saw the Los Angeles Aqueduct Cascades, a part of the Los Angeles Aqueduct built to bring water from Owens Valley, California to Los Angeles. William Mulholland, Chief Engineer for the City of Los Angeles Bureau of Water Works and Supply, directed construction of the aqueduct. The aqueduct, begun in 1908 and completed in 1913, extended for 233 miles from the Owens River in the eastern Sierra Nevada Mountains to Los Angeles., A triumph of engineering, the water in the aqueduct flowed downhill all the way with no pumping required.

75. The Los Angeles Aqueduct Cascades near Sylmar. (The water cascades down the open channel on the left, although some also comes down the pipeline on the right.)

In the 1920s, oil was being pumped from numerous fields around the Los Angeles area. In some places, especially around Long Beach and Signal Hill, the small property lots allowed oil wells to be so close to one another that the derricks were nearly touching. Some of the outlying areas learned from this and placed more restrictions on the spacing of the wells.

76. Widely spaced oil wells near Los Angeles, including several along the hilltops.

Catalina Island is a rocky island 22 miles southwest of Los Angeles in the Gulf of Santa Catalina. In 1919, William Wrigley, Jr., of chewing gum fame and owner of the Chicago Cubs baseball team, bought controlling interest in the company that owned Catalina Island. Wrigley's efforts to turn the island into a tourist mecca included having the Chicago Cubs use Catalina Island for spring training starting in 1921. These efforts were still big news around Los Angeles, and Roy decided the Crawfords should take the trip across the Gulf to see the island while they were in the area. One day they dressed in their best clothes and went to the Catalina Island terminal in Los Angeles harbor to board the SS Avalon, the passenger steamer that made the trip to Catalina Island daily. Each round-trip ticket cost $2.43 and the trip across lasted 2 hours and 15 minutes.[43] Kansas was far from any ocean, so none of the Crawfords had ever been sailing on the ocean before and this "ocean voyage" was a new and exciting adventure. When they arrived at the harbor at the town of Avalon on the island, they found it to be a sleepy little community with a population of only a few hundred, and they soon realized that there was not a lot to do there.

77. Clarence, Pauline, Albina, and Roy dressed for a trip to Catalina Island on the SS Avalon seen in the background.

---

[43] This ticket price is equivalent to about $36 in today's dollars, so this trip was quite an expenditure for the Crawfords—no wonder they wore their good clothes!

78. Avalon Bay on Santa Catalina Island with the SS Avalon on the right belching smoke.

79. The harbor at Avalon Bay on Santa Catalina Island.

They did discover Sugarloaf Rock, a bullet-shaped outcrop at the end of Sugarloaf Point, which formed one end of Avalon Bay. The first casino at Avalon (a dance hall and meeting place, not a gambling place) was built adjacent to Sugarloaf Rock in 1919. A much larger casino, completed in 1929, replaced the original one razed in 1928. Sugarloaf Rock had a very steep wood ladder running up its side. Climbing at least part way up this ladder would have been fun for Clarence and Pauline, but unfortunately there was a sign posted there saying that climbing on the ladder or the rock was strictly forbidden by the Santa Catalina Island Company.[44]

The Crawfords spent a few hours on the Island and then traveled on the ship Avalon back to Los Angeles. The "ocean voyage" there and back was probably the best part of the trip to Catalina Island.

80. Sugarloaf Rock on Santa Catalina Island.

---

[44] Sugarloaf Rock no longer exists. In the 1930s, it was destroyed by blasting to improve the ocean view seen from the Avalon Casino.

The Crawfords spent considerable time in Riverside, named for its location beside the Santa Ana River. Founded in the early 1870s, Riverside became the birthplace of the California citrus industry in 1873 when three Brazilian navel orange trees were planted there. The trees flourished in the local climate and soil, and by 1882 there were more than half a million citrus trees in California, nearly half of which were in Riverside County.[45] Orange groves filled the area. By 1922, the population of Riverside had reached about 20,000.[46]

Albina wanted to pick oranges in the groves alongside the road, but Roy didn't want her to do it since they didn't belong to her. When they finally stopped to pick some, the owner came out and they "took off fast," according to Pauline. Later they managed to pick oranges in many different places, and enjoyed being able to eat them whenever they wanted.

---

[45] Citrus is no longer the dominant economic driver in the Riverside and Redlands areas that it was when the Crawfords were there. With the rise of urbanization in Southern California, what was once the state's original "citrus belt" has gradually migrated north into the San Joaquin Valley.

[46] By 2010, the population of Riverside had increased 15-fold, to about 300,000.

81. Orange trees covered to protect from frost.

82. Clarence, Albina, and Pauline in front of an orange grove.

83. Pauline and Clarence picking oranges from a tree, with some help from Roy.

*84. Pauline and Clarence with
oranges in Redlands, a town
near Riverside.*

White Park, established in 1883, was Riverside's first city park. It included a cactus garden, a rose garden, a bandstand, and a canal, making it a pleasant place to visit. Even though it was wintertime, it was great to be able to sit outside at the bandstand in lightweight clothing and listen to a concert.[47]

---

[47] White Park now bears little resemblance to what it was when the Crawfords were there. Alterations after 1931 changed White Park's setting from one of tree-lined streets and orange groves to that of an urban area. These alterations included the removal of the cactus garden, demolition of the bandstand, and filling in of the canal that flowed diagonally through the park.

85. The cactus garden in White Park.

86. Roy, Pauline, Clarence, and Albina at the cactus garden in White Park.

Just east of Riverside is Mount Rubidoux, a popular tourist destination. Father Junipero Serra, the founder of some of the earliest Spanish missions in southern

California, supposedly frequently travelled through the valley and often rested at Rancho Rubidoux. A large wooden cross and a tablet, erected at the top of the mountain and dedicated in 1907, honored Father Serra. This cross was made of tree logs and stained brown.[48] Of course, the Crawfords had to get into their good clothes to climb up there and have their picture taken.

87. Minnie, Albina, Clarence, Pauline, Charlie, and Roy at the Father Junipero Serra cross on Mt. Rubidoux.

The Glenwood Mission Inn in Riverside was a famous hotel where social leaders, celebrities, and even U.S. presidents and other political figures had stayed. The original adobe boarding house, built in

[48] Mount Rubidoux would look very different now. A Testimonial Peace Tower and World Peace Bridge were dedicated there in 1925. In 1963, the original wooden cross, damaged by vandals, was replaced with a white, hollow-core cement cross that looks nothing like the original.

1876, was called "The Glenwood Cottage." In the early 1900s California's citrus boom and warm weather attracted wealthy travelers and investors, and the Cottage blossomed into a full-service hotel named "The Glenwood Mission Inn." In 1902, the owner started building an eclectic structure. Architecture included Spanish Gothic, Mission Revival, Moorish, Spanish Colonial, Spanish Colonial Revival, Renaissance Revival, and Mediterranean Revival. The Crawfords went there prepared to look and be impressed, but they did not intend to stay there overnight.

88. Glenwood Mission Inn.

On one trip, the Crawfords drove up to Big Bear Lake near San Bernardino. Bear Valley was dammed in 1884 to create Big Bear Lake, a reservoir for irrigation in the Redlands area. A new multiple-arch dam, completed in 1912, increased the capacity of the lake. This latter dam had a small walkway extending over the tops of some of the arches.[49] By the 1920s, Big Bear Lake had become a popular resort area with facilities for camping and fishing. The family probably camped there for a night or two, since Roy couldn't pass up a chance to fish.

89. Crawfords on the walkway across Big Bear Lake Dam.

---

[49] A highway bridge across the tops of these arches replaced this walkway later in 1923.

The family spent Christmas in Riverside. Roy's mother, Candus Crawford Norris, and her new husband Jack Norris came out on the train from Kansas to join them there. They all sat down to Christmas dinner in the campground where they were staying.

90. Roy, Clarence, Albina, Minnie, Charlie, Jack Norris, Candus Crawford Norris, and Pauline enjoying Christmas dinner at their campground in Riverside.

Pasadena, incorporated as a city in 1886, grew in population from about 9,000 in 1900 to about 30,000 in 1910—enough to service several new grand hotels. Through the end of the 1920s, Pasadena continued to enjoy a reputation as a tourist center and winter resort for the wealthy. The population of Pasadena was about 50,000 in 1923.[50]

---

[50] The population of Pasadena had increased to about 140,000 by 2010.

One of the many impressive things in Pasadena was the Colorado Street Bridge, noted for its arches and railings and for the electric light standards along its length. Colorado Street was the major east-west thoroughfare connecting Pasadena with Glendale to the west and Monrovia to the east. This bridge, completed in 1913, is nearly 1,500 feet long with a maximum height of 150 feet. It spans the Arroyo Seco, a big canyon that cuts through the middle of Pasadena, passing the Rose Bowl Stadium and running through Brookside Park. In the rainy season, a river runs through the Arroyo.

91. The Colorado Street Bridge over the Arroyo Seco.

Adolphus Busch (brewer of Budweiser beer) purchased the house "Ivy Wall" overlooking the Arroyo Seco in Pasadena in 1905 to have a place to spend winters in a warmer clime. He developed the arroyo behind the house into a lush walking garden, and he continued to purchase land behind the house so that he eventually ended up with over 30 acres of gardens. Adolphus died in 1913 and the house and gardens passed to his wife Lily. The Crawfords spent some time exploring and admiring these gardens, which were still a major tourist attraction in the early 1920s.[51]

92. The Adolphus Busch winter home "Ivy Wall."

In 1890, the Valley Hunt Club held a mid-winter festival in Pasadena featuring a procession of flower-covered horses and carriages. The Tournament of

---

[51] The Busch house and gardens are gone now. Upon Lily's death in 1928, the gardens were closed to the public and they were later sold off and subdivided for homes. The City of Pasadena refused to preserve the Busch home and the house was razed in 1952. Only a few remains of the rock walls and the garden structures can still be seen.

Roses Association took over the festival in 1898, making it an annual tradition. The Crawfords timed their visit to Pasadena specifically to attend the Rose Parade on New Year's Day. They all went to see the parade in the morning and Pauline and Clarence picked up crepe paper there after the parade had passed. In the afternoon, Roy went to the football game in the newly opened Rose Stadium; this was the first Rose Bowl Game to be played in this stadium and the stadium was officially dedicated at that game on January 1, 1923. The University of Southern California Trojans defeated the Penn State Nittany Lions 14-3. The stadium had a distinctive horseshoe shape at that time (in 1928, the open end was filled in to make it a true bowl). The next day all the floats from the parade gathered in the stadium for a public viewing, and the family went there get a close look at them.

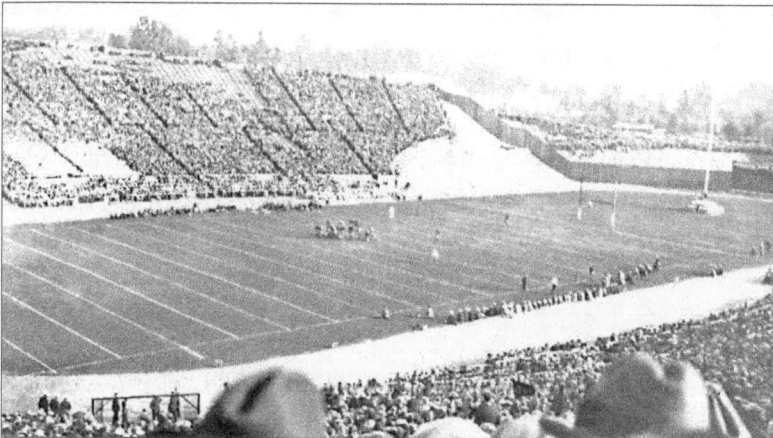

93. First Rose Bowl Game played in Rose Stadium

Brookside Park was right next to the Rose Stadium. It had many recreational facilities, including baseball fields used for spring training by the Chicago Cubs from 1917 through 1921 and by the Chicago White Sox in the 1930s. The Crawfords watched a baseball game there, but the teams were not identified.

94. Baseball diamonds at Brookside Park in Pasadena.

The family could see Mount Wilson from Pasadena. It wasn't a particularly interesting peak except that the famous Mount Wilson Observatory was located there. That observatory regularly made news since it housed what at the time was the world's largest telescope. Edwin Hubble used the telescopes there throughout the 1920s to make many notable discoveries about galaxies outside the Milky Way.

95. Baseball game at Brookside Park.

96. Mount Wilson

As the Crawfords were getting ready to leave the Los Angeles area, they made a side trip to Palm Springs,[52] a resort area about 55 miles east of San Bernardino. Palm Springs has a hot desert climate with over 300 days of sunshine per year and an average annual rainfall of 4.8 inches. However, there is a plentiful supply of water from the various hot

---

[52] Map site 15.

springs there. In the 1900s, health tourists began arriving with conditions that required dry heat, and the city became a fashionable resort. The Desert Inn in Palm Springs was established as a hotel and sanitarium in 1909, but the next major hotel there was not built until 1924. The population of Palm Springs was only about 3,000 in 1923.[53]

Pauline and Clarence had the same impression of Palm Springs—it had palms and a spring and that was about it.

97. Palm Springs, California.

---

[53] The Palm Springs area has seen enormous changes since the Crawfords were there. The population of Palm Springs had increased to about 45,000 in 2010. The annual number of visitors to Palm Springs and the surrounding area increased 60-fold, from about 200,000 in 1923 to about 12,000,000 in 2010.

98. Minnie, Charlie, and Pauline at Palm Springs.

January to April: the San Diego Area

The Crawfords backtracked from Palm Springs to San Bernardino, to take the road south through Riverside and Escondido to San Diego[54]. This part of the trip was only about 186 miles and the road was paved for most of the route. They enjoyed this scenic trip through orange groves and mountains. Finally, in mid-January the travelers reached San Diego, which would be their home for the rest of the winter and into early spring.

San Diego has been called the "Birthplace of California."[55] Juan Rodriguez Cabrillo, the first European to land on what is now the West Coast of the United States, landed in San Diego Bay in 1542 and claimed the area for Spain. San Diego became part of the newly independent Mexico in 1821, and became part

---

[54] Map site 16.

[55] *City of San Diego and San Diego County: the birthplace of California*, Clarence Alan McGrew, American Historical Society, Chicago and New York, 1922.

of the United States in 1848. The original settlement of San Diego, now known as "Old Town," was located away from the bay, but in the late 1860s, people and businesses began to relocate to the bayside area of "New Town," which became downtown San Diego. Once the railroad arrived in 1878, San Diego began to grow rapidly. The U.S. Navy presence in San Diego began to grow in 1901 and expanded significantly in the 1920s. The city, an early center for aviation, also proclaimed itself "The Air Capital of the West." Tourism has long been a major industry for San Diego due to its mild year-round climate, natural deep-water harbor, and extensive beaches. By 1923, the population of San Diego had grown to about 90,000.[56]

In San Diego, the travelers camped in the Municipal Camp Grounds in Balboa Park. The cost was 50 cents a night for each vehicle and the camp contained all the conveniences for "roughing" it: a grocery store, a community kitchen and dining room, showers, a steam laundry, outdoor furniture, and a community building. Campers supplied music for dances held in the community building.

---

[56] By 2010, the population of San Diego had increased 14-fold, to about 1,300,000.

99. Postcard of the Municipal Camp Grounds in San Diego.

In the top year of 1923, 40,000 persons came to the camp in 10,000 vehicles from every state in the Union and five foreign countries. While the Crawfords were there, several of the other campers were living in camping vehicles similar to the Crawfords' RV.

100. *A variety of designs displayed ingenuity for constructing camping vehicles.*

Best of all for Pauline and Clarence, there were many other kids there with ample opportunity for play and activities.

101. *Kids posing in front of yet another "RV" at that campground.*

102. *Boys playing in a mud puddle near the Balboa Park Campgrounds.*

103. *Clarence with other children in front of the Crawford RV, wearing paper hats they had made.*

Boxing, planned or perhaps occurring spontaneously, seemed to be a popular form of entertainment in the camp.

104. Boys boxing at the Balboa Park Campgrounds.

This looked like so much fun that the women decided to try it too.

105. Women boxing at the Balboa Park Campgrounds.

This campground was a wonderful place for an extended stay, and the Crawfords met and made a number of friends there.[57] A group picture was one way to remember them.

106. Roy (second from left), Charlie, and Minnie (Charlie standing and Minnie sitting just right of the car roof), posing with a group of people staying in the campground.

The campground was located in Balboa Park, a 1,200-acre urban cultural and recreational park in San Diego. Created in 1835, Balboa Park is one of the oldest public recreational parks in the United States.

---

[57] This was a great location and very successful as a campground, but you can't camp there now. The Municipal Auto Camp in Balboa Park existed only from 1920 through 1924; after that, the camp was closed to make way for an expansion of the San Diego Zoo.

This park hosted the San Diego portion of the 1915 Panama-California Exposition, and many of the buildings and facilities there were constructed for that Exposition. The California Bell Tower, the Cabrillo Bridge, Spreckles Organ Pavilion, and the San Diego Zoo were among those. Much of the park landscaping dated from then as well. The zoo was close to the campground and was free for children, so Clarence and Pauline often walked there.

Cabrillo Bridge, a historic pedestrian and automobile bridge, was built to provide access across Cabrillo Canyon between Balboa Park and the Uptown area of San Diego. It was primarily intended for pedestrian access to the Exposition and during the time of the Exposition auto traffic was allowed only for dignitaries.

The California Bell Tower (also known as the California Tower) is part of the California Quadrangle and the California Building, which housed an anthropological display called "The Story of Man through the Ages," the Exposition's theme exhibit. After the Exposition ended, the exhibit eventually became the San Diego Museum of Man.

107. California Tower and Cabrillo Bridge in Balboa Park.

Spreckles Organ Pavilion houses the open-air Spreckles Organ, the world's largest pipe organ in an outdoor venue. John D. Spreckles, son of a sugar magnate and one of the wealthiest people in San Diego, provided funding for both the pavilion and the organ.

108. A concert at Spreckles Organ Pavilion in Balboa Park.

109. Pauline, Albina, and Clarence with two other couples under a palm tree at Balboa Park.

One of the very best things about San Diego was the Pacific Coast near La Jolla, a community within the city of San Diego located north of the Downtown area. The Crawfords went there many times. There were great rock formations with waves breaking over them, along with many sandy beaches to play on. They could also find seashells and could study the marine life in tidal pools. Best of all it was warm enough to go there at almost any time even though it was mid-winter.

110. Looking for shells on the beach at La Jolla.

111. Alligator Head formation at La Jolla.[58]

---

[58] This Alligator Head formation can no longer be seen. The arch in the rock formation collapsed in 1978 due to ocean erosion and storms, and the rest of the landmark fell in 1983.

112. Minnie, Albina, Pauline, and Clarence at the La Jolla coast.

113. Clarence and Pauline playing in the surf with a friend.

114. Pauline, Albina, Minnie, Clarence, and Roy digging for clams at low tide.

Ramona, an 1884 American novel by Helen Hunt Jackson, was set in Southern California.[59] The novel became immensely popular and had a considerable influence on the culture and image of Southern California. Its publication coincided with the arrival of railroad lines in the region, resulting in countless tourists who wanted to see the locations in the novel. In 1887, a front-page article in the *San Diego Union* declared that the Casa de Estudillo, a historic adobe house constructed by Jose Maria Estudillo in 1827, was "Ramona's Marriage Place." In 1906, the San Diego Electric Railway Company purchased and renovated the dilapidated building so it more closely matched descriptions in the novel. Upon its completion in 1910, it was marketed to tourists

---

[59] *Ramona*, Helen Hunt Jackson, Little, Brown, 1884

as "Ramona's Marriage Place," and it remained popular as such for years to come.

Whether or not the Crawfords had read the novel, they got dressed up and went to see Ramona's Marriage Place because it was famous.[60] The building didn't seem that special, but there were a few interesting things around it.

115. Roy, Albina, Clarence, Minnie, Pauline, and Charlie at Ramona's Marriage Place.

---

[60] "Ramona's Marriage Place" is gone now. In 1968 the Casa de Estudillo, which had long been marketed as "Ramona's Marriage Place," was donated to the State of California. The state Park Service then restored the building to its pre-Ramona days. The house now serves as a museum and all traces of its former association with Ramona have been removed. The old Spanish caretta that was at Ramona's Marriage Place is now displayed at The Seeley Stable, a restored building in Old Town San Diego State Historic Park.

116. Pauline, Roy, Clarence, Charlie, and a friend from the camp, pose around the 400-year-old Spanish caretta (ox cart) at Ramona's Marriage Place.

117. Albina admiring a cactus at the Cactus Garden at Ramona's Marriage Place.

The establishment of the Navy Coaling Station on Point Loma in 1901 marked the beginning of significant naval presence in San Diego. This was followed by the introduction of the Marine base Camp Matthews on a mesa in La Jolla in 1917, the commissioning of the Marine Corps Recruit Depot San Diego in 1921, and the San Diego Naval Training Center in 1923. The Camp Mathews site was later turned over to the University of California, San Diego in 1964.

Naval Base San Diego was established as U.S. Destroyer Base San Diego in 1922, and the San Diego Naval Hospital was established then as well. In the early 1920s, the destroyer base was the home for active, reserve, and mothballed destroyers and served as a fleet repair facility. The destroyer base grew rapidly, and in 1924, they decommissioned 77 destroyers and commissioned seven, reflecting the fact that the navy was modernizing and scaling back after WWI. The Crawfords would occasionally go down to the bay to see the mothballed destroyers and to watch the active ships steaming in and out of the harbor.

The battleship Pennsylvania visited San Diego from February 2 through February 8 in 1923, and the Crawfords went to the harbor to see her while she was there. Launched in 1915, she was the lead ship of the Pennsylvania class of super-dreadnought battleships that were a modest improvement over the preceding Nevada class. After her launch, the Pennsylvania participated in training exercises off the east coast of the U.S. until late 1921, when she sailed through the Panama Canal and up to her new home port in San Pedro harbor at Los Angeles.[61]

118. Battleship Pennsylvania at San Diego.

---

[61] The battleship Pennsylvania remained active throughout World War II. By 1941 the Pennsylvania was based at Pearl Harbor, and on December 7 she was in dry dock there undergoing a refit. The dry dock prevented the Pennsylvania from receiving major damage during the Japanese attack on Pearl Harbor, and she later went on to participate in numerous battles across the Pacific. After the war, she participated in the nuclear tests at Bikini Atoll, where she became heavily contaminated. After a period of study of the radiation effects, she was deliberately sunk in a deep part of the Pacific.

119. Battleship Pennsylvania and a destroyer.

120. Destroyer steaming in the bay.

121. Mothballed destroyers.

On one occasion, the Crawfords were able to see an air show with the airplanes flying in formation and doing aerobatics. This air show originated from North Island, which was commissioned as Naval Air Station San Diego in 1917. The Navy shared North Island with the United States Army's Signal Corps, Air Service. Aviation milestones originating at North Island included the first seaplane flight in 1911, the first parachute jump in 1914, the first mid-air refueling in 1923, and the first non-stop transcontinental flight, also in 1923.

122. Biplane flying upside down at the air show.

123. Planes flying in formation at the air show.

San Diego was also a significant port for shipping, including passenger ships bound for foreign ports. The Crawfords could watch the shipping activity when they went down to the dock area. Broadway Pier, the first of San Diego's reinforced concrete piers built on the bay, was one of the main piers there. Built in 1913, the Broadway Pier serviced passenger vessels until its replacement in 2010.

124. A passenger ship at the Broadway Pier.

The family also watched loading operations on the passenger-cargo vessel Californian, docked at another pier. The Californian was built in 1922 by Merchant Shipbuilding Corporation, an American company established in 1917 by railroad heir W. Averill Harriman, and was intended for use on Harriman's American-Hawaiian Line.

125. The recently built freighter Californian docked in San Diego.

Tijuana, Mexico is just across the border from San Diego. When the Crawfords drove there just to look around, they found the streets crowded with cars. Prohibition in the U.S. occurred from 1920 to 1933, and because there was no prohibition in Mexico, the bars in the Mexican towns close to the U.S. flourished during that time. This was especially true in Tijuana, with the booming city of San Diego having a large U.S. naval contingent just across the border. The population of Tijuana was about 100,000 in 1923, similar to that of San Diego at that time.[62]

---

[62] By 2010, the population of Tijuana had increased 13-fold, to about 1,300,000. ("MEXICO: Baja California", http://citypopulation.de/Mexico-BajaCalifornia.html)

126. Minnie, Clarence, and Pauline standing in line along a busy street in Tijuana.

On a different excursion, they took a boat trip across the border and around the Mexican Coronado Islands, just offshore from Tijuana. The Coronado Islands are a group of four islands about eight miles off the northwest coast of Baja California, and are part of the municipality of Tijuana, Mexico.

127. Coronado Islands in the Pacific Ocean near Tijuana.

128. Feature in the Coronado Islands.

Occasionally the Crawfords ventured into the countryside near San Diego. One trip took them to Sweetwater Dam, about 12 miles east of San Diego. This dam, which impounds Sweetwater Reservoir on the Sweetwater River, was first built in 1888 to provide water for San Diego and other towns in the area, as well as irrigation water for crops. The dam was retrofitted several times over the ensuing years, and both abutments had to be replaced in 1916 after they failed in a heavy flood.

129. Sweetwater Dam east of San Diego.

In the spring, not too long before they left San Diego, they made a trip to an almond orchard. The almond trees were in bloom and made a pretty sight. Almonds were planted in California as early as 1853. Almond production in California increased steadily into the 1920s. Even though it was recognized early that irrigated almonds produced larger crops, growers did not start to apply irrigation water until the 1930s. The Central Valley then became the main area for almond production in California, but at least into the 1930s there were still some almond orchards near San Diego as well.

130. Pauline and Clarence at an almond orchard.

The Road Home:

April to June

San Diego to Yuma
(~194 miles)

Finally, the time came to leave San Diego and start the trip back to Kansas. The Crawfords were sad to leave their new friends at the Balboa Park campground, but they missed their farm and their friends and relatives and were ready to head home.

The Dixie Overland Highway, part of the Old Spanish Trail in this area, took them east across the southern edge of California, crossing the border into Arizona at Yuma. After leaving San Diego, the road climbed to the summit of the coastal range, an elevation of 4,100 feet. This portion of the road was partially paved and partially gravel. Primitive ferries rather than bridges provided crossings for many streams and rivers. These typically consisted of a one-vehicle-sized barge that was pulled across the river by a rope or cable. You drove onto the barge, and then the ferry attendant used the rope to pull the barge with you and your vehicle across the river. If the ferry attendant wasn't there when you arrived, you were out of luck and had to wait until he showed up.

131. A basic ferry for crossing a small river.

132. The RV and Charlie and Minnie's car along the Dixie Overland Highway in San Diego County.

The road from San Diego to Yuma served enough travelers to sustain gas stations and other travel-supported facilities. The RV stopped at this garage for gasoline, and Roy took advantage of the stop to carry out some minor repairs, using the tools stored in the box seen mounted under the RV.

133. Repairing the RV at a garage along the Dixie Overland Highway in San Diego County.

From the summit of the coastal range, about seven miles of dirt and stone road made the steep descent through walls of rocks and canyons into the Imperial Valley, a part of the Sonoran Desert that is almost all below sea level. The valley extends from the edge of San Diego County all the way to the Arizona border and into Mexico. The soil there is very good for agriculture, but the average annual rainfall is only about three inches, so except for irrigated spots, the valley is all desert.

134. The desert in the unirrigated parts of the Imperial Valley is mostly a monotonous flat panorama.

135. Hills occasionally punctuate the desert, adding some diversity to the landscape.

In 1923, irrigation water from the Colorado River was available over some parts of the valley. The Crawfords wanted to see these irrigated farming operations since they involved crops such as winter fruits and vegetables, cotton, grain, and alfalfa. Most of these were different from the crops grown in Kansas and required different methods of farming including much more hand labor.

136. Farmland ditched for irrigation in the Imperial Valley.

*137. Pauline in orchard with young date palms in the
Imperial Valley.*

138. Pauline and Clarence at a cotton field in the Imperial Valley.

139. Farm workers in the Imperial Valley.

El Centro, California was a major farming center in the Imperial Valley. While there, the Crawfords visited the city of Mexicali,[63] the capital city of the Mexican state of Baja California. Mexicali was a small farming

---

[63] Map site 17.

center with a population of about 9,000, just across the border into Mexico.[64]

140. Popular street in Mexicali, Mexico.

---

[64] Mexicali is now a major manufacturing center, and by 2010, its population had increased 77-fold, to about 690,000. ("MEXICO: Baja California", http://citypopulation.de/Mexico-BajaCalifornia.html)

141. Roy, Pauline, Albina, and Clarence in Mexicali. Despite what the sign says, they probably were not there for the dancing.

East of El Centro, they entered an area of the desert marked by shifting sand dunes. Vehicles had to navigate an eight-foot-wide plank road with some wider spots for other vehicles to pass. The plank road provided a firm footing for the vehicles, but it was still a challenge to cross.

"Tourists must make local inquiries before attempting to cross the desert, as the route may be impassable. Before starting this trip see that your gas tank is filled to capacity and have an extra supply of water and provisions. Useful implements are shovel and hand axe. Immediately after crossing Highline canal deflate tires and be sure to get them soft enough for good flat surface. Keep car moving and stay in the rut. Do not let wheels spin or jump – if they do instantly ease up on the throttle until

such action ceases. In case your car gets stuck in the sand cut some brush and lay it crosswise for wheels to track on." — *Automobile Blue Book, p. 853.*

After they made it through this part of the desert, they crossed over the bridge spanning the Colorado River into Yuma, Arizona.

142. Midday in the desert; Minnie, Clarence, and Pauline on the bleak expanse of sand dunes in the Imperial Valley.

Yuma to Phoenix (~219 Miles)

Yuma, Arizona is located on the Colorado River border with California. The early settlements in the area combined and took the name Yuma in 1873. As one of the few natural spots to cross the Colorado River, Yuma soon became the gateway to Southern California, and in the late 1800s people crossed the river there on ferries as part of the Southern Emigrant Trail. Yuma had a population of about 4,300 when the Crawfords passed through there.[65] Surrounded by the Sonoran Desert, Yuma is very dry and very hot. It has an annual average of 3.36 inches of rain, and has a maximum temperature of at least 90° F on nearly half the days of the year.

The Dixie Overland Highway led the family from Yuma through the Sonoran Desert, roughly following the Gila River to Gila Bend, Arizona. At Gila Bend, they left the Dixie Overland Highway and proceeded toward Casa Grande, Arizona. The Blue Book had this

---

[65] The population of Yuma had grown to about 93,000 by 2010.

to say about the stretch of road from Yuma to Gila Bend.

> *"First 35 miles is over newly constructed gravel highway; balance of trip is over rough, unimproved sandy dirt roads. The route follows the Gila River valley through level desert country surrounded by rugged mountain ranges. Except for a few ranches there is no habitation beyond Wellton and tourists are advised to carry extra water and supplies." —Automobile Blue Book, p. 853.*

The Crawfords' pictures indicate how empty and desolate this area was. They also indicate some of the different kinds of challenges posed by desert "roads."

*143. Ruts served as part of the route through the
desert between Yuma and Casa Grande.*

The Blue Book did not cover the route they took
from Gila Bend through Maricopa to Casa Grande. A
Rand McNally map from the 1920s describes this
route as a "dirt or poor road," and the Crawfords'
pictures demonstrate what that meant. This road was
as bad as or worse than the road they had just left at
Gila Bend. However, they did manage to find an
"oasis," which was a popular stopping place with a
campground and a store that presumably had food,
water, and gasoline for sale.

144. Desert road and "oasis" (actually a store and a campground) on the route from Yuma to Casa Grande.

145. RV negotiating the challenging roadway, following the ruts across a gully. Charlie and Minnie were right behind them.

146. RV traversing another challenging spot on the route from Yuma.

The family went to Casa Grande to see the nearby Casa Grande Ruins National Monument. [66] This Monument preserves a group of structures constructed by the Sonoran Desert people who developed wide-scale irrigation farming and farmed the Gila Valley in the early 13th century.

A compound wall surrounded the ruins at Casa Grande. Casa Grande or "big house" refers to the largest feature on the site, which is what remains of a large building that was probably abandoned prior to 1450. Made of caliche using traditional adobe processes, the big house consists of three-story-high outer rooms surrounding a four-story inner room. [67]

---

[66] Map site 18.

[67] Caliche is a naturally occurring sedimentary rock made of materials such as gravel, sand, silt, and clay bound together by calcium carbonate.

Some repair and preservation activities at Casa Grande began as early as 1891, and the external shelter shown in the Figures 148 and 149 was built in 1903. President Woodrow Wilson declared Casa Grande a National Monument in 1918.

147. Ruins at Casa Grande. The person standing in the front provides a sense of the scale of the building.

148. The "big house" at Casa Grande. Pauline and Albina are peeking out from inside.

From Casa Grande they drove north into Phoenix over a good road, partially graded gravel, and partially paved. Yavapai County first recognized Phoenix as a town in 1868, and Phoenix got its first post office shortly thereafter. By the mid-1870s, Phoenix had a telegraph office, sixteen saloons, four dance halls, and a population of about 2,000. It became a trade center when the railroad arrived in the 1880s, and by 1900, the population had risen to about 5,500. Phoenix became the state capital when Arizona was admitted to the Union in 1912, and its population continued to increase, reaching about 35,000 by 1923.[68]

When the travelers arrived near Phoenix they headed east on the Apache Trail Highway[69] through the Superstition Mountains to Roosevelt Dam and the Tonto National Monument. The 81-mile long Apache Trail Highway, the wildest and most dangerous road the Crawfords experienced, was especially challenging for the RV.[70]

---

[68] The population of Phoenix had increased 40-fold, to about 1,400,000 in 2010.

[69] Map site 19.

[70] Unlike most other roadways the Crawfords traveled, the Apache Trail road is remarkably almost the same now as when the Crawfords were there. It remains largely unpaved and limited to one lane in places. Some large RV rental companies in the U.S. refuse to allow their vehicles to be taken on this route.

"Pavement to Mesa; then dirt and gravel to edge of valley, followed by 30 miles of rocky road thru mountains; fair road from Fish Creek Sta. to Roosevelt Dam; . . . Thru a rich irrigated district to a point 5 miles east of Mesa, entering a wild and rugged mountain country 23 miles beyond. Long grades and many sharp curves demand slow and careful driving." —Automobile *Blue Book, p. 854.*

149. Campground at the entrance to a canyon on the Apache Trail Highway

A recent Arizona travel brochure gave this description of the Apache Trail Highway:

"The Apache trail is characterized by magnificent geological/rock formations and steep-sided canyons rising high into the sky. For several miles along the way you'll find the Four Peaks Wilderness rising directly to

the north and the Superstition Mountains Wilderness directly to the south. At one point you'll be hugging the side of Fish Creek Canyon, high on a sheer wall dropping hundreds of feet below (and there's a 2-mile stretch of one-lane gravel road here)."

"Heading east from the western end of the Apache Trail you'll be rising above the desert through a series of hairpin turns with some great views out over that Sonoran Desert landscape below. Then you'll follow the canyon cut by the Salt River between the Mazatzal Mountains and the Superstitions past the Goldfield ghost town, past Lost Dutchman State Park, then past Canyon Lake and Apache Lake until you come into the area around Theodore Roosevelt Lake."[71]

The Superstition Mountains, largest of the mountain ranges surrounding Phoenix, are characterized by sheer-sided, jagged, volcanic peaks and ridges separated by boulder-filled canyons. The name Superstition arose from the myths and stories told by the local Pimas and Apaches about the mountains. The name is also linked with tales such as the fabled Lost Dutchman's gold mine, reportedly a

---

[71] *Apache Trail Historic Road,*
http://www.sangres.com/arizona/scenic-byways/apache-trail-historic-road.htm

mother lode found in the Superstition Wilderness by a German immigrant who died before he could reveal the location of the mine.

150. On the Apache Trail Highway, through the Superstition Mountains.

151. The terrain in the Superstition Mountains was very rugged. Barely visible in the picture, the road winds its way through this canyon.

152. Crawford families sheltering in the shade along the canyon walls at Fishing Creek Grade.

153. The RV heading down the canyon wall at Fishing Creek Grade on the Apache Trail Highway.

154. Stopping to stretch while ascending a canyon wall on the Apache Trail Highway.

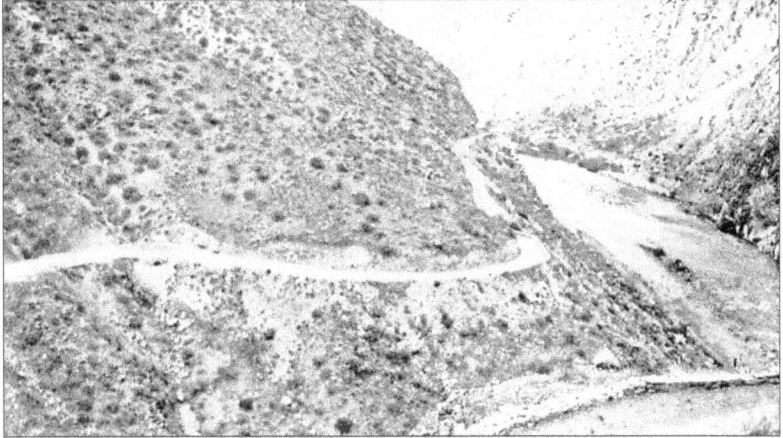

155. Apache Trail Highway as it winds along the Salt River near the Roosevelt Dam in Arizona.

Roosevelt Dam and Lake were the goals at the end of the trip on the Apache Trail Highway. The Crawfords camped at Roosevelt Lake for several days, giving them time to rest before making the trip back along the Apache Trail Highway to Phoenix. Rising 280 feet, Theodore Roosevelt Dam[72] was built between 1905 and 1911. It formed Theodore Roosevelt Lake intended to serve mainly for irrigation and flood control, but the dam also had a hydroelectric capacity of 36 megawatts. Roosevelt Lake covers much of the southern portion of the Tonto Basin; the Sierra Ancha Mountains, the Mazatzal Mountains, and the Superstition Mountains surround it. Smallmouth bass were introduced into the lake in the early 1920s, and it has been known as a great fishing spot ever since. Pauline and Clarence used a bent pin on a string to

[72] Map site 20.

fish there, but despite their efforts, they couldn't catch anything. The rest of the family was probably more successful, since they had better fishing equipment.[73]

156. Roosevelt Dam, northeast of Phoenix

---

[73] Roosevelt Dam and Lake now look quite different from when the Crawfords were there. An ambitious expansion and renovation project, begun in 1989, completely encased the original rubble-masonry dam in concrete, significantly changing its looks. At the same time, the structural height of the dam was raised from 280 feet to 357 feet, adding to the depth and surface area of the lake.

157. Roosevelt Dam and Lake.

*158. Spillway and power plant at
the Roosevelt Dam.*

159. Campsite at Roosevelt Lake

While at Roosevelt Lake, the Crawfords made a side trip to Tonto National Monument, which was within sight of the lake. The Monument comprised remains of two cliff-dwelling complexes and associated prehistoric and protohistoric cultural sites. People of the Salado culture inhabited these cliff dwellings for approximately 300 years, until they abandoned the area for unknown reasons around 1450 A.D. The two-story Lower Ruin originally had 19 rooms, and most of these are well preserved. Originally, the only access was by ladder leading to an entrance at the far left of the structure. The Upper Ruin is larger with 40 rooms, but is more remote.

The Crawfords spent some time walking around the Lower Ruin; the Upper Ruin was much more difficult to get to, so they didn't go up there.

160. Lower Ruin cliff dwelling at Tonto National Monument.

161. Front view of the Lower Ruin cliff dwelling at Tonto National Monument.

Following their stay at Roosevelt Lake, the Crawfords retraced their route back to Phoenix, where they camped at Papago Saguaro National

Monument.[74] This Monument was created in 1914 to preserve the "splendid examples of the giant and many other species of cacti and the yucca palm, with many additional forms characteristic of desert flora that grow to great size and perfection and are of great scientific interest, and numerous prehistoric pictographs of archeological and ethnological value."[75]

The Monument was named for the saguaro cacti, a tree-like cactus species that can grow to over 40 feet tall. These cacti are native only to the Sonoran Desert, which extends over much of Southern Arizona, the Mexican state of Sonora, the Whipple Mountains, and the Imperial County areas of California. Early Sonoran Desert people living in this region marked the changing seasons and predicted seasonal events by monitoring the movement of the sunlight through a formation there now known as Hole-in-the-Rock. This was a popular tourist spot, and some of the previous visitors had already carved their initials inside this formation. The Crawfords found the Hole-in-the-Rock to be a great place to sit in the shade and look out across the miles of desert covered with cacti.

---

[74] Map site 21.

[75] President Woodrow Wilson's 1914 proclamation creating the Papago Saguaro National Monument.

162. Charlie, Clarence, Roy, Pauline, and Minnie at Hole-in-the-Rock.

163. Papago Saguaro National Monument had an expanse of saguaro cacti and sagebrush as far as the eye could see.

164. Saguaro cacti.

165. Clarence, Albina, Pauline, Minnie,
and Charlie with Minnie and Charlie's car
parked under a large saguaro cactus.

Another plant native to this area is the ocotillo (*Fouquieria splendens*). This plant, which appears to be a collection of spiny dead sticks for much of the year, quickly becomes lush after a rainfall and can retain its small leaves for several weeks. Individual stems can reach a diameter of 2 inches at the base, and the plant may grow to a height of over 30 feet.[76]

166. Albina, Pauline, and Clarence with an ocotillo plant.

---

[76] Papago Saguaro National Monument no longer exists. In 1930, the National Monument designation was removed and the land ownership was transferred to the state and local governments, primarily because lack of funding had prevented even the basic preservation and management tasks so that the area was being degraded by the influx of tourists who stole plants and left graffiti. Figure 167 shows an example of such degradation that had already happened by 1923. A small portion of the area that was Papago Saguaro National Monument, including the part with the "Hole-in-the-Rock," became a municipal park of the cities of Phoenix and Tempe, Arizona.

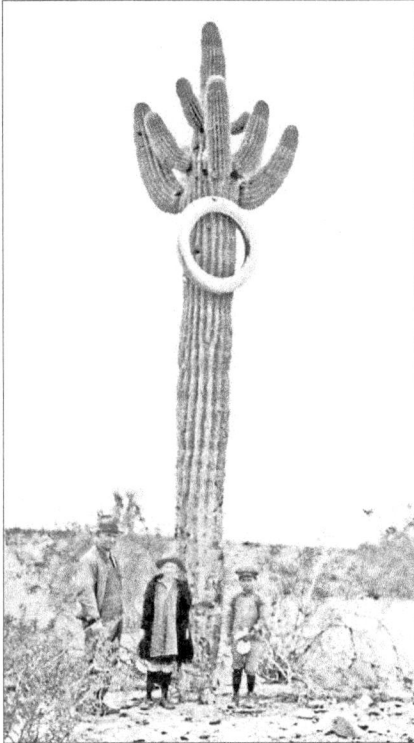

167. Roy, Pauline, and Clarence next to a saguaro cactus. The spare tire might have been someone's idea of a joke. Probably not so funny for whoever had to climb up there.

Phoenix to Grand Canyon National Park (~249 miles)

Heading north from Phoenix on the Black Canyon Road, the travelers started out in a desert climate near Phoenix, but along the way, they climbed more than 4,000 feet in altitude, moving into a mountainous terrain and climate with the corresponding changes in weather. This road followed an old stage route to Prescott Arizona and passed through scenic mountain country with some very steep grades.

> *"First 8 miles macadam, then rough road to Bumble Bee Station, fair road to Dewey, balance graded gravel and dirt."—Automobile Blue Book, p. 600.*

About 50 miles north of Phoenix, they passed Turret Peak, a small mountain with a peak elevation of 5,794 feet. Located in Yavapai County in Tonto National Forest, it is noted for the battle of Turret Peak, a turning point of one of the largest campaigns in Arizona to quell the fights between settlers and the native Yavapai and Apache. The Tonto Basin campaign was organized in 1871 and the goal was to force the native population to return to the reservations. In March 1873, a group of Yavapai and Apache were camped on Turret Peak, which they thought would be a safe place. However, a small unit of Army scouts crept silently up the sides of the peak and attacked the natives at dawn. Fifty-seven natives died as a result and several more were wounded and captured. This defeat so demoralized the Yavapai and Apache people that most of them allowed themselves to be peacefully returned to their reservations.

The travelers took a picture of this peak because of its strange shape that stood out from its surroundings.

168. Turret Peak, about 50 miles north of Phoenix.

From Prescott they followed the Grand Canyon–Nogales Highway north to Ash Fork, then east to Williams and finally north again to the South Rim of the Grand Canyon.

The Grand Canyon, carved by the Colorado River in Arizona, is a steep-sided canyon 277 miles long, varying from eight to 20 miles in width, and reaching a depth of about 5,000 feet measured from the South Rim. The South Rim has an average elevation a little over 7,000 feet, and has semi-arid flowering vegetation. From April to November the southern rim is free from snow.

The Grand Canyon and nearby areas became a National Park in 1919.[77] In 1920, the National Park enclosed 958 square miles and included 56 miles of the Grand Canyon stretching west from its beginning at the mouth of the Marble Canyon. By 1920, a branch of the Atchison, Topeka & Santa Fe Railroad extending 64 miles north from Williams, Arizona, reached the South Rim of the Park. The South Rim could also be reached by automobile either from Williams or from Flagstaff, Arizona, which is about 34 miles east of Williams. In 1920, there was one hotel on the South Rim: the El Tovar named for the Spaniard who first discovered the canyon. The El Tovar was located at the railroad terminus and was open all year with rates of $6-$8 per person. The Park had about 100,000 visitors in 1923.[78]

---

[77] Map site 22.

[78] Annual attendance at Grand Canyon National Park increased from about 100,000 in 1923 to about 5,000,000 in 2010.

The Crawfords stayed at the free public campground near Grand Canyon Village that was available to campers. The Park allocated camp sites free of charge, by application to the superintendent of the park. A garage in the village provided gas and oil; a grocery store sold groceries, but campers were encouraged to bring a supply with them. Water for drinking, bathing, and automobile radiators had to be hauled by rail to the park, since there was no local supply. Visitors either had to bring their own water with them or else to purchase water in the village.

The roads in the park carried a mix of automobiles, motorcycles, horse or mule drawn vehicles, horse or mule riders, and hikers. Park regulations limited automobile speeds to 12 miles per hour on grades and around sharp curves, to 20 miles per hour on straight stretches when no team was within 200 yards, and to eight miles per hour when passing any animals on the road. Animals had the right-of-way, and automobiles had to take the outer edge of the roadway to make way on the inner edge whenever teams, saddle horses, or pack trains approached. All automobiles had to carry at least one spare tire and to have their brakes in good shape.

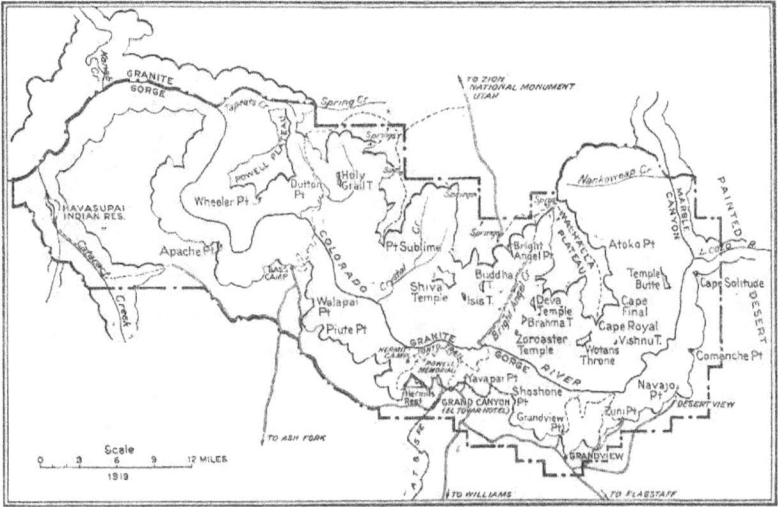

169. 1920 Map of Grand Canyon National Park.

170. Roy and Pauline look at a book, while Clarence rests under a tree at the public campground near Grand Canyon Village.

171. Charlie and Minnie with their tent at the campground.

*172. Grand Canyon with the Colorado
River flowing through it.*

173. Grand Canyon and Colorado River.

Hopi House, a reproduction of the dwellings of the Hopis, was built before 1920 and was located opposite the El Tovar hotel. It contained collections of native handiwork, and a small band of Hopis lived there.

174. Hopi House.

In 1869, Major John Wesley Powell led the first expedition to travel down the Colorado River through the Grand Canyon. A memorial, approved in 1909 and dedicated in 1918, commemorates the trip. It stands at Powell Point, about three miles west of Grand Canyon Village. You can see from the family's clothes that it was chilly when they were there—not surprising since it was spring and the elevation was about 7,000 feet.

175. *Clarence, Albina, Charlie, Minnie, and Pauline at the Powell Memorial.*

Roy took the mule trip down Bright Angel Trail to the bottom of the Canyon, which in this area was about 4,500 feet below the rim of the canyon.[79] The cost was $5.00 per person. The trip down was seven miles, and it was a "much longer" seven miles back up. This would normally be a very strenuous two-day trip for hikers, but the use of the mules relieved much of the strain, making it possible to go down and back in a single day. The trip was still very tiring, but the views along the way made it worthwhile. They left on the mules at 8:30 AM and were back at 5:30 PM.

---

[79] The Bright Angel Trail generally follows the Bright Angel Fault, and is one of the main trails at the Grand Canyon. The first four miles descend steeply via a series of switchbacks. After about the four-mile point, the trail levels out and heads along a wide bench beside a deeper ravine for about a mile and a half before it begins to make another steep descent through a rugged area known as the Devil's Corkscrew. The last half mile to the river at the bottom of the canyon is relatively level.

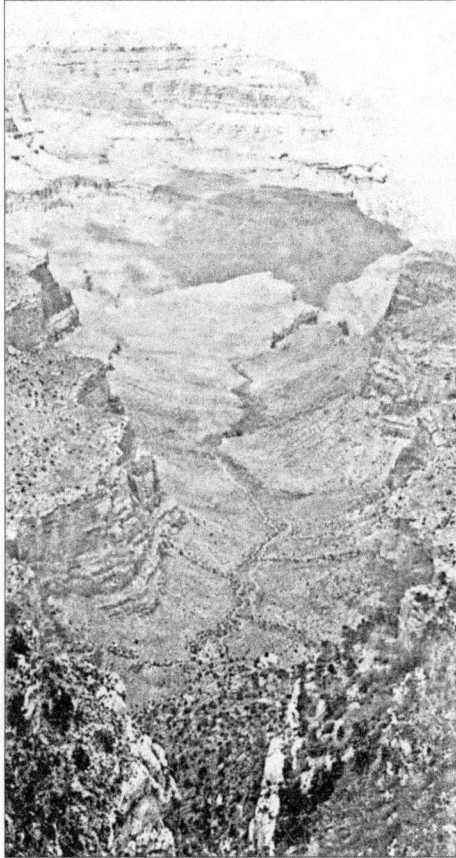

*176. Bright Angel Trail becomes visible
in this picture as it follows the
relatively smooth terrain down the
middle, before making its final
descent to the Colorado River*

177. Roy starting the mule trip to the bottom of the Grand Canyon.

178. Everyone dismounted and walked, with staff leading the mules, along this part of the trail.

179. Mules and riders at the bottom of the Grand Canyon.

180. Roy resting by the river at the bottom of the Grand Canyon. He may have had one of the trip staff take this picture

181. View from the bottom of the Grand Canyon.

The rest of the family settled for a ride on the bridle paths along the rim of the canyon.

182. Riding on the bridle path along the South Rim.

Grand Canyon National Park to Petrified Forest National Monument (~187 miles)

From the Grand Canyon, the Crawfords took the road down to Flagstaff. This road was rated as a "fair to good prairie road, with a few bad stretches of sand and rock." They were used to bumpy roads by this time, so this was no problem. From Flagstaff they headed east on the National Old Trails Road, a stretch that later became part of Route 66. Looking back, they could see Humphreys Peak, the highest point in Arizona at 12,633 feet.

183. Humphreys Peak near Flagstaff, Arizona.

Further down the road they arrived at Walnut Canyon National Monument, located about 10 miles southeast of downtown Flagstaff, close to the National Old Trails Road. The elevation at the Walnut Canyon rim is 6,690 feet and the canyon's floor is 350 feet lower. The Sinagua, a pre-Columbian cultural group, lived there from about 1100 to 1250 A.D. and constructed cliff-dwelling rooms in the walls of the canyon. Walnut Canyon was proclaimed a National Monument in 1915 to protect those dwellings. Sinagua is Spanish for "without water," and the Sinagua people became experts at conserving water and dealing with droughts. The Sinagua built their homes under limestone ledges deep within the canyon, taking advantage of the natural recesses in the limestone walls. These dwellings were small but they provided adequate space for the inhabitants to cook and sleep. The Crawford family spent some time exploring these ruins.

184. Visitors on the trail in front of the cliff dwellings.

185. Albina walking in front of the cliff dwellings.

The travelers continued east along the National Old Trails Road from Walnut Canyon to the Petrified Forest National Monument[80] near Holbrook, Arizona. The Petrified Forest area was designated a National Monument in 1906 and became a National Park in 1962. The area consists of semi-desert shrub steppe

---

[80] Map site 23.

and highly eroded colorful badlands. It averages about 5,400 feet in elevation and has a dry windy climate. Temperatures vary from summer highs of about 100 degrees to winter lows well below freezing. Average precipitation in the spring is about one-half inch per month.

The Petrified Forest is known for its fossils, created about 225 million years ago during the late Triassic Period. At that time, downed trees accumulating in river channels were buried by sediment that included volcanic ash containing silica. This silica formed quartz crystals that gradually replaced the organic matter in the logs. These quartz crystals incorporated traces of iron oxide and other substances from the sediment to produce the varied colors in the petrified wood. Some of these trees were up to 300 feet long and at least six feet in diameter.

Prior to the 1930s, there were virtually no public facilities and no roads (other than the National Old Trails Road/Route 66) in the Petrified Forest National Monument. Since there were no public facilities or roads, the Crawfords drove wherever they wanted and camped wherever they found a good place. When they got there they found an area to use as their campsite, and after Charlie fixed his tent, they set up camp.

186. Charlie works with their tent while Minnie surveys the landscape at the Petrified Forest National Monument.

187. Camping in a random open space at the Petrified Forest.

Then it was time to look around. It was fantastic! There were petrified logs lying all over the place and Clarence and Pauline could run around looking at all of them and climbing on the interesting ones. They especially liked to look at the varied colors in the petrified wood. There were few, if any, other people there, so the Crawfords had the place more-or-less to themselves.

188. Minnie photographing a petrified log. The RV and Charlie and Minnie's car are in the background.

189. Clarence, Roy, Albina, Pauline, and Charlie on and by a large petrified log.

190. Pauline, Charlie, and Clarence inspecting a petrified log.

191. Pauline, Minnie, Albina, and Clarence standing on petrified logs. The hills in the distance are part of the Painted Desert.

192. Roy, Pauline, Charlie, Clarence, and Albina with petrified logs.

*193. Charlie, Minnie, Clarence, Pauline, and Albina on
a large petrified log.*

Although they weren't supposed to disturb anything in the monument, Albina did pick up a small piece of petrified wood, which they hid away in their camper until they reached home. They used it as a doorstop in their Kansas farmhouse and it was still there many years later for their grandchildren to play with, a reminder of a remarkable trip.[81]

---

[81] The Petrified Forest site has become a major tourist destination since the Crawfords were there. The Civilian Conservation Corps built roads, structures, and trails in the monument between 1934 and 1942. During this same period, additional land in the Painted Desert section was added to the Monument. In 1962, the Monument became the Petrified Forest National Park. Annual attendance at Petrified Forest National Park had grown to nearly 700,000 by 2010. Visitors are now restricted to marked trails, paths, and observation areas in the most popular areas, and are not allowed to spend the night in the main parts of the park.

Petrified Forest to Santa Fe (~406 miles)

The National Old Trails Road led east-northeast from the Petrified Forest, crossing the border into New Mexico near Lupton, Arizona and continuing generally eastward to Los Lunas, New Mexico. The road then turned and proceeded north through Albuquerque and on to Santa Fe. The topography along this part of the route led to a roadbed characterized by climbs, descents, switchbacks, and cuts, passing through a mountainous area with several long stretches of rolling prairie. The roadway was either gravel or dirt since none of it was paved until after 1923.

"The distances are great between points, tourists are advised to keep supplies of provisions replenished." —Automobile Blue Book, p. 775.

"Graded gravel and dirt roads predominate on this trip. Some rough stretches crossing dry river beds. . . Use

caution on turns and also use horn freely."
—Automobile Blue Book, p. 775

Along the way, they saw several different native pueblos. Shortly before reaching Albuquerque, they stopped at the Isleta Pueblo[82] located on the Rio Grande River in the Middle Rio Grande Valley, 13 miles south of Albuquerque. In the 1920s the National Old Trails Road passed next to it. Established around 1200 A.D., it is home to the Tiwa tribe. The Spaniards named the pueblo Isleta ("little island"). During the eighteenth and nineteenth centuries, Isleta was noted for its crops and orchards, and it became one of the most prosperous pueblos in New Mexico. The original church in the pueblo was rebuilt in 1716 and was named St. Augustine. The St. Augustine Mission, still standing today, is one of the oldest in the United States. In the 1920s, Isleta was the largest of the Rio Grande pueblos, numbering over one thousand inhabitants. Unlike at some other pueblos, the houses in Isleta Pueblo were a single story high, so the many buildings required to house all the inhabitants spread out over a large area.

---

[82] Map site 24.

194. Old weathered adobe in Isleta Pueblo.

195. An Isleta Pueblo adobe exhibiting a more recent style.

196. Street scene.

The family continued northward through Albuquerque, past the Santo Domingo Pueblo and on to Santa Fe. By far the most famous set of switchbacks on this stretch of roadway was the ascent from the plains up the side of La Bajada Mesa just before reaching Santa Fe. These switchbacks were constructed largely with the use of convict labor. The old wagon trail up the side of the mesa had a grade of 28% in places, and this was reduced to a maximum grade of 7.5% with the construction of the switchbacks, making it accessible to automobiles. These switchbacks were quite intimidating to many motorists, and enterprising locals would offer to drive their cars down the hill for them for a fee. An early 1920s sign at the bottom of the hill read:

LA BAJADA HILL
Warning
Safe Speed 10 Miles
Watch Sharp Curves
This Road Is Not Fool Proof
But Safe For A Sane Driver
Use Low Gear

This no doubt inspired confidence in the Crawfords as they headed up the hill. Roy may have taken this as a challenge, but their drive up La Bajada Hill was probably less frightening than a trip down that hill would have been.[83]

197. La Bajada Hill on the National Old Trails Road south of Santa Fe.

Once they made it up the hill, it was only a short distance into Santa Fe. New Mexico's second Spanish governor, Don Pedro de Peralta, founded Santa Fe in

---

[83] These switchbacks are no longer available to test the nerves of the drivers. The original road up La Bajada Hill was abandoned in 1932 when a new route was laid out a few miles further east.

1607. In 1610, he designated it the capital of the province. Even after the U.S. acquired the New Mexico Territory in 1848 under the Treaty of Guadalupe Hidalgo, Santa Fe remained the capital, making it the oldest state capital in the U.S. In the early 1900s, the Santa Fe civic leaders enacted a plan that anticipated limited future growth due to the scarcity of water. This plan established the principle that historic streets and structures must be preserved and that new development must be consistent with the city's character. The beauty of the landscapes, its dry climate, and the cultural richness of the area attracted artists, writers, and retirees to Santa Fe, and the town gradually developed as a tourist attraction. The city sponsored architectural restoration projects and erected new buildings according to traditional techniques and styles and the city began to grow. In 1923, Santa Fe had a population of about 7,300.[84]

The travelers spent several days in Santa Fe, enjoying the Spanish architecture and the other sights there.

---

[84] The population of Santa Fe was about 70,000 in 2010.

198. Burro carrying firewood in Santa Fe.

La Fonda means "the inn" in Spanish. The La Fonda hotel on the Plaza in Santa Fe was built in the early 1920s on a site that had been the location of various inns since 1609. This hotel was designed and built in the "Pueblo Revival Style" and was hailed as "the purest type of Santa Fe architecture and . . . one of the most truly distinctive hotels anywhere between Chicago and San Diego."[85]

---

[85] *All Aboard for Santa Fe: Railway Promotion of the Southwest, 1890s to 1930s.* Victoria E. Dye, Albuquerque, University of New Mexico Press, 2007.

199. Albina, Clarence, and Pauline in front of the La Fonda Hotel.

Native Americans were selling a variety of native crafts in the Plaza at Santa Fe, and the Crawfords got some of them to pose at their RV.

200. Native American family posing with Clarence and Albina beside RV. The artisans are holding small pots that were for sale to the tourists there.

Santo Domingo Pueblo, named by the Spanish conquistadores in the 17th century, was located approximately 25 miles southwest of Santa Fe along both the railroad and the National Old Trails Road.[86] By the early 1920s, it had become a major tourist destination, and was as close to "Indian country" as many tourists could get. [87] The people of the community reacted by producing pottery and jewelry specifically for the tourist market.

The Crawfords bought a native pottery vase for 25 cents while on their trip. This piece of pottery is polychrome and exhibits the distinctive bird and floral designs frequently found on Santo Domingo pottery. A member of the Santo Domingo Pueblo probably made it. The Crawfords may have purchased their pottery along the road as they passed through that Pueblo, but it is also possible that they purchased it in

---

[86] This portion of the National Old Trails Road became part of Route 66 in the mid-1920s.

[87] "Indian country" was the term historically used to refer to territories beyond the frontier of settlement that were inhabited primarily by Native Americans. The term was still in common use in the 1920s to harken back to the days when such territory had been in sometimes violent dispute.

Santa Fe, since Native Americans from the Santo Domingo Pueblo often sold their wares there.[88]

201. Two views of the Native American vase the Crawfords purchased for 25 cents. This vase is about 8½ inches tall.

Jesus Sito Candelario's "Original Old Curio Store," created shortly after the turn of the 20th century by combining two old adobe commercial buildings, has long been a Santa Fe landmark. All the merchandise displayed in the windows invited the travelers in to look around.

---

[88] In 2009, the Santo Domingo Pueblo officially changed its name back to the local name in their Keres language, and it is now known as Kewa Pueblo.

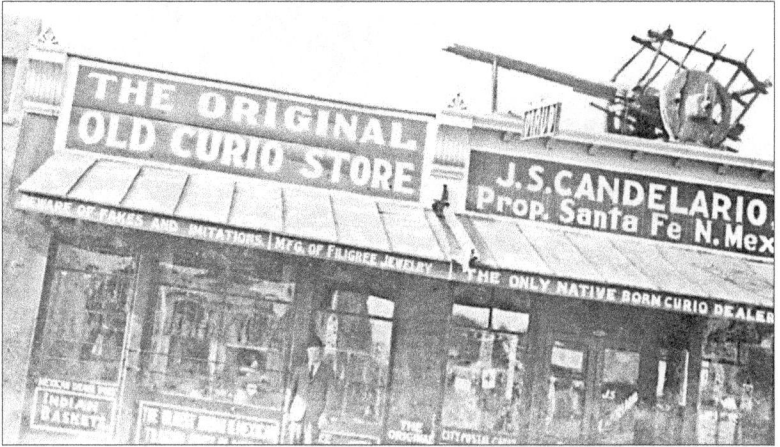

202. Roy in front of the Old Curio Store. The camera was tilted to include the cart on the roof in the picture.

The New Mexico Museum of Fine Arts (later the New Mexico Museum of Art) is the oldest art museum in the state. Built in 1917, it is an example of Pueblo Revival Style architecture.

203. Charlie and Minnie's car (front vehicle) and Pauline, Albina, and Clarence in front of the New Mexico Museum of Fine Arts.

San Miguel Mission, built between approximately 1610 and 1626, is the oldest known church in the continental U.S. Repaired and rebuilt over time, the church retains its original adobe walls, now partially hidden by later additions.[89]

---

[89] The San Miguel Mission underwent a major restoration in 1955, and now is in much better shape than when the Crawfords were there.

204. San Miguel Mission in Santa Fe, the oldest known church in the continental U.S.

Santa Fe to Home (~613 miles)

From Santa Fe, the travelers continued to follow the National Old Trails Road (this stretch was also known as the Mountain Route of the Santa Fe Trail), east to Las Vegas, New Mexico. From there they headed north-northeast through Raton New Mexico, over Raton Pass (elevation 7,834 feet), and across the Colorado border to Trinidad, Colorado. The only major towns between Santa Fe and Trinidad along this route were Las Vegas and Raton, each with a population of about 5,000, but the road passed through a number of smaller towns as well. Most of this road was rated as improved, although a short stretch was rated only as graded. In many places, it was hardly more than a trail and some places were very poor and rocky. The road through Raton Pass in the 1920s provided its share of switchbacks, steep grades, and cliffside driving.

The Crawfords stopped for the night in Trinidad, situated 13 miles north of the Colorado-New Mexico border at an elevation of 6,025 ft. in the Purgatoire River valley. There they posed for an "end of trip" picture. Compared with Figure 4 taken prior to starting the trip, Albina and Roy now exhibit none of the quiet sense of anticipation seen in the "before trip" picture, and appear somewhat travel weary instead. Pauline looks a lot more sophisticated; after all, she had a birthday while on the trip and is a much older and more experienced ten-year-old now. Clarence appears to have grown a little taller, and looks like he wishes they were already home.

205. Albina, Clarence, Roy, and Pauline with RV in Trinidad.

From Trinidad, they followed the National Old Trails Road on past La Junta, Colorado to near Lamar, Colorado where their route jogged about 25 miles north to catch the road they took at the start of their trip. That route led them back through Leoti, Kansas, and on to their farm.

Back Home at Last!

They had been away from home for nearly ten months by now, roughly half of which had been spent in Southern California—in San Diego and in the Los Angeles area. This period in Southern California had the desired effect; Albina's respiratory problems had disappeared and her health was now much improved. As a bonus, the family had experienced a memorable extended educational adventure.

Their trip had taken them through majestic mountain, desert, and coastal scenery. They had marveled at remarkable technological achievements: huge hydroelectric dams, graceful automobile bridges, massive ocean liners, and at least two of the country's largest battleships. The family had made new friends from different parts of the country. The RV had faithfully taken them over some of the most challenging and gut-wrenching mountain roads in the country and through some of the most desolate regions of the nation. They had also spent time in some of the lushest areas in America. Their trip had involved more than 5,000 miles of driving at about 15 miles per hour or less, taking their Model T RV

206. Home again! The Crawford farmhouse in the early 1920s.

through conditions ranging from well-paved roadways to one-lane mountain roads and routes that were a series of random ruts.

Bill Hampl had been operating the farm for them while they were away, and he had everything in great shape when they returned. He was glad to see them back, and they were delighted to be back and able to sleep once again in real beds in their own home. After having been gone a long time, they were tired of traveling and of living in the RV. Many wonderful memories of the trip would linger, but it felt good to be home again.

Besides, it was almost time for the next wheat harvest!

Epilogue

The spirit of adventure, love of learning, and self-confidence that propelled the Crawford family on their remarkable 1922-1923 expedition remained with them after they returned. They went on to lead productive lives, and to have many other travel adventures, although none of these later adventures was quite as extraordinary as their 1922-1923 trip. Nevertheless, their continued appreciation of both education and travel was apparent throughout the rest of their lives.

Roy and Albina

After arriving back home from this trip, Roy and Albina and their children returned to living in their same farmhouse. Roy resumed farming, and continued to be successful, while acquiring additional land in the late 1920s, again in the 1930s, and a final piece of land in the 1940s. By the late 1920s a tractor had replaced the teams of horses for some of the farm work. They continued to live frugally in their farmhouse, only occasionally adding a few amenities.

In the late 1940s and early 1950s, Clarence helped install a propane tank, a floor furnace, and a gas range to replace the coal stove used to heat the house and the kerosene-burning kitchen stove used for cooking. They were not able to install a pump system and indoor plumbing until the 1950s, when the REA (Rural Electrification Administration) finally brought electricity to the area.

However, Roy and Albina still felt the urge to get out and see other places, frequently making excursions together with Crawford and Hampl family members and other friends. They made numerous camping trips to Colorado, including visits to Mesa Verde and to Grand Mesa, and traveled to see some of the sights in Texas in the late 1930s. They also made occasional trips to Nebraska to visit Hampl relatives and to Oregon to visit Myrtle Thomas.

In the early 1950s, Roy and Albina bought an Airstream travel trailer, and began spending winters in McAllen, Texas along with several other couples from the Luray area. They varied their routes to and from McAllen to allow them to visit many other regions of Texas. By the mid-1950s, they and the other Luray couples switched their winter quarters from McAllen to Punta Gorda Florida, and they continued to winter there throughout the remainder of the 1950s.

Roy Crawford died in 1960. He was 78 years old. After his death, Albina moved out of their farmhouse, spending some of her time in a house in Luray, and some of her time with Clarence's family in Russell. Albina died in 1963 at the age of 76.

Pauline

In the years following the trip, Pauline continued her education through the eighth grade at the Amherst school. After that, she attended high school in Luray. Luray was seven miles from their home, so it was no longer practical for her to walk to school. Instead, several parents from their local community formed a car pool, taking turns driving all their high-school-age students to Luray each morning and back home later in the day. After completing high school, Pauline attended Kansas State College (later, University) in Manhattan, Kansas, which was unusual for women at this time and a testament to the value placed on education by the family. She graduated in 1934 with a degree in Home Economics. Manhattan was just over a hundred miles from their farm, so frequent trips back and forth were out of the question. Pauline lived on campus, taking the train back to Luray a few times but usually being driven to and from college by her parents.

When the World's Fair was held in Chicago in 1933, Pauline, Clarence, and two of their friends convinced their parents to allow them to drive to Chicago to attend the Fair. They went in the family car belonging to the parents of their friends, and traveled under strict instructions not to exceed 35 miles per hour. They had a great time, managing on their own to handle lodging arrangements and meals along the way and at the fair.

In 1938, Pauline accepted a job as a Home Demonstration Agent in Stafford County, Kansas, and she lived in the town of St. John in that county.[90] In 1945, she married Dale Bookstore, a farmer and rancher from St. John. Dale's first wife had died, leaving him with two young children, and Pauline became their stepmother. They lived on Dale's farm just outside St. John, and Pauline was active in numerous community organizations. In later years, Pauline and Dale made several trips to the Pacific Northwest to visit their daughter's family. After Dale's death in 1996, Pauline continued to live in St. John, and received the title "Lady of the Year" in 2000 for her many years of community service. She remained heavily involved in community activities as long as she was able, and at the age of 90, she was still coordinating a series of fund-raising teas for the community. Pauline died in 2012, 98 years old at the time.

---

[90] Home Demonstration Agents were county representatives of the Department of Agriculture, employed to teach many different homemaking skills throughout the community. Typical skills might include planning healthy meals, safe canning, sewing, and even money management.

Clarence

Clarence followed Pauline's example educationally. He completed the eighth grade at the Amherst school, and then went on to high school in Luray. He also attended Kansas State College, where he majored in Agricultural Engineering, graduating in 1937. He participated in the ROTC program while in college, earning him a commission of Second Lieutenant in the Army. However, there was no room for additional officers in the peacetime army when he graduated, so he went back to farm with his father. He married Gladys Chegwidden in 1939, and they lived in the farmhouse that had been the home of his grandmother Candus Crawford Norris.

In 1941 Clarence was called to active service as a First Lieutenant in the Army Coastal Artillery as the U.S. prepared for possible entry into World War II, and he and Gladys traveled to Georgia and then to North Carolina where he began training with his unit. I was born while they were stationed in North Carolina. In early 1942, Clarence's unit shipped out to the Pacific, where they would spend the next two and a half years defending air bases in Australia and New Guinea.

After returning from overseas with the rank of captain, he was assigned to a training unit at Fort Bliss, and he and his wife and son spent the next year living in El Paso, Texas. By the end of the war, he had completed his five years of service, and he was discharged in early 1946. Later in 1946, he and Gladys had another child, my sister Candace Ruth Crawford.

After the hiatus caused by the war, Clarence was able to get back to farming. He modernized the farmhouse where he and Gladys had previously lived and the family moved into it. He gradually took over most of the farming operations on his father's land. He served on the school board for the Luray school system for a number of years, and was president of the board for much of this time. He was also active in other Luray community activities. A few years later, the Kansas governor appointed him to the Kansas State Board of Education, where he served for six years, two of those as the board president.

In 1962, Albina came to live with Clarence's family, and the family moved to Russell where she could be closer to medical care. Clarence continued to farm, however, making the seventeen-mile commute daily on most days of the year. He continued to farm until retiring in the late 1980s, at which point he leased the farm land to another operator. In the mid-1960s, he and Gladys took an extended trip to Europe, visiting distant relatives there and touring through many countries. After he retired, they had more time for travel and he and Gladys embarked on an extensive series of tours to Western Europe, Scandinavia, Russia, the Middle East and Northern Africa, South America, and Australia. In Australia, they were able to revisit some of the areas where Clarence was stationed during the war. Between these tours, they also traveled to visit their children and grandchildren in New Jersey, Los Angeles, Illinois, Boston, and San Francisco.

After long, eventful, and productive lives, Gladys died in 2002 at the age of 92, and Clarence passed away in 2008 also at the age of 92.

The RV

The 1922-1923 Crawford trip occurred during the early stages of an exponential increase of automobile travel. By the mid-1920s, the existing, somewhat haphazard, system of roadways had been made part of a national highway plan, and the quality of the highways began to improve at a much faster pace. The Crawfords' RV as well as the other home-built mobile homes seen on their trip was in the vanguard of the accompanying rapid increase in the use of automobiles for tourism and other recreational purposes. Automobile manufacturers soon began producing their own lines of vehicles designed for camping. This became the beginning of an industry. The large and luxurious house trailers and RVs common today can rightly be viewed as descendants from those early home-built mobile homes.

As to the Crawfords' RV itself, it does not appear in any of the numerous pictures the Crawfords continued to take subsequent to their monumental trip. Pauline and Clarence couldn't remember what happened to that RV, and no record can be found to indicate whether the Crawfords ever used it again for travel. It is possible that the RV cabin was removed so the truck chassis could be adapted as a useful farm vehicle, but there is no record of that either. It is also possible that they sold it "as is" to someone else who had an immediate need for such a vehicle for their own travels. This missing chapter in the history of the Crawfords' RV will continue to be one of the remaining mysteries of the album found in Dad's attic.

The Farm

The Crawford farm remained in the family, and in 2001, it was awarded the status of Century Farm by the Kansas Farm Bureau, recognizing that it had been owned and operated by the same family for more than 100 years. Homesteaded by Harmon and Candus Crawford, the farm was acquired and expanded by Roy and Albina, and later owned and farmed by Clarence and Gladys. I grew up on that farm, and when I was old enough, began operating the farming equipment there. It gave me great satisfaction to be the fourth generation of Crawfords to till those fields and to harvest the grain from them. The farm is still owned by the Crawford family descendants, and is currently farmed by a Hampl relative, a direct descendant of one of Albina's siblings.

My Journey into History

This journey into history that began with the discovery of an album in Dad's attic has led me through a previously unknown portion of my family's history, and along the way has provided a glimpse into a slice of time when life still proceeded at a more leisurely pace. This was a time when the American West was still in the early stages of its period of phenomenal growth, and looked far different than it does now. Since that time, America has gained population, technology, infrastructure, and expertise over the intervening century, but the competence, courage, self-confidence, and yearning for adventure displayed by our ancestors has survived and flourished.

Dad's attic is now empty of Crawford artifacts, all the travelers on this remarkable trip are gone, and I have traveled as far as I can into this particular piece of history. This journey of mine has now reached its conclusion. It has been an extremely satisfying journey, and I am already looking forward to my next exploration.

Acknowledgements

The encouragement and advice I received from my wife, Charlotte Crawford, was essential to the creation of this book. She convinced me to turn my collection of research notes about the Crawford Album into a book, and then provided the editorial and publishing guidance essential to make this book into a reality. Thanks to her, the final product is far better than anything I could have produced on my own.

Post Rock Press skillfully carried out the layout of this book, a task made difficult by the large numbers of photographs to be included and properly positioned in the text. The staff there carried out this tedious work cheerfully, and with excellent results.

Our daughters, Lara Crawford and Clare Crawford are keen on participating in new adventures. They volunteered with alacrity to read this manuscript. Their valuable comments, suggestions, and questions led to clarification of numerous passages in the book, and provided an opportunity to educate them on their farm heritage.

Finally, thanks are also due to my father, Clarence, and my aunt, Pauline, who, while they were still alive, were able to remember enough information about this trip they experienced as children to provide the initial stimulus and guidance for this project.

Bibliography

Rand McNally auto road atlas of the United States and Ontario, Quebec, and the maritime provinces of Canada, with a brief description of the national parks and monuments. Rand McNally & Company, Chicago, 1927. California State Library David Rumsey Historical Map Collection. https://www.davidrumsey.com

A Year in the West: A Kansas Family's Expedition. Pauline Crawford Bookstore and Clarence Crawford, as told to R. Kent Crawford, Candace Crawford, and Charlotte Anderson Crawford. CrawforDesign, Knoxville, TN, 2000.

Western and Transcontinental Automobile Blue Book, 1922, Volume 4. The Automobile Blue Books, Inc. New York, NY, 1922.

Rules and Regulations: Yellowstone National Park. Washington, Government Printing Office, 1920. https://www.nps.gov/parkhistory/online_books/broch ures/1920/yell/index.htm

Rules and Regulations: Grand Canyon National Park. Washington, Government Printing Office, 1920. https://www.nps.gov/parkhistory/online_books/brochures/1920/grca/sec1.htm

Internet sources were used extensively to identify the location and contents of many of the Crawfords' photos.

Population values cited for U.S. locations throughout this book were based on U.S. census data. At the time of this writing, the most recent census data available was from the 2010 census.

Media Credits

All the figures in this book are from photographs in the Crawford Album, except for the following:

1: The route of the Crawford trip is sketched atop a 1927 Rand McNally road map, courtesy of Rand McNally.

2: Photograph courtesy of the R. K. Crawford family.

5: Based on photographs courtesy of the Candace Crawford family.

6: Photograph courtesy of the R. K. Crawford family.

7: Photograph courtesy of the R. K. Crawford family.

20: Map courtesy of Yellowstone National Park: brochure *Yellowstone NP: Rules and Regulations (1920),* Government Printing Office, Washington D.C., 1920.

46: Souvenir Postcard found among Crawford mementos from the trip. Courtesy of the R. K. Crawford family.

58: Souvenir Postcard found among Crawford mementos from the trip: Pacific Novelty Co., San Francisco. Courtesy of the R. K. Crawford family.

99: Souvenir Postcard pasted in the Crawford album. Courtesy of the R. K. Crawford family.

169: Map courtesy of Grand Canyon National Park brochure: *Yellowstone NP: Rules and Regulations (1920),* Government Printing Office, Washington D.C., 1920.

201: Photographs courtesy of the Candace Crawford family.

Author photo by Michael Broyles Photography.

About the Author

R. KENT CRAWFORD grew up in the house built by his great grandmother on the central Kansas farm that his great grandparents homesteaded in the late 1800s. After attending public school in the nearby town of Luray, he obtained a bachelor's degree in physics from Kansas State University and a PhD in physics from Princeton University. He spent his professional career primarily at Argonne National Laboratory and at Oak Ridge National Laboratory, authoring numerous technical articles and book chapters. He is a Fellow of the American Physical Society. Since his retirement, he has amused himself by researching and writing articles about various aspects of his family's history. This is his first non-technical book.

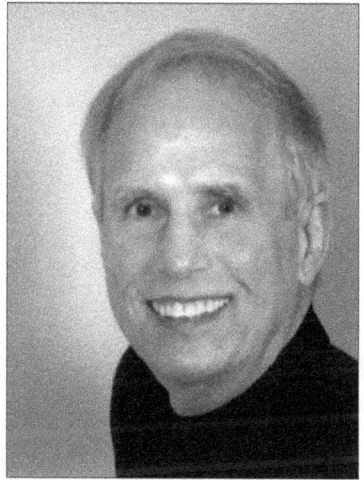

www.ingramcontent.com/pod-product-compliance
Lightning Source LLC
La Vergne TN
LVHW041315080426
835513LV00008B/468